Spiritual Springboard

Your Spiritual Guide
To
Knowing God Personally

By

Pamela Evischi
spiritualspringboard.com

Scriptures taken from the Holy Bible, New International Version®, NIV®, Copyright © 1973, 1978, 1984 by Biblica, Inc.™ used by permission of Zondervan,
All rights reserved worldwide.

NIV Quest Study Bible

Published by Zondervan

Grand Rapids, Michigan 49530, USA

Copyright© 1994.2003,2011 by Zondervan

ISBN-13: 978-0-578-46535-7

All rights reserved. This book may not be reproduced in whole or in part, or transmitted in any form, or by any means electronic, mechanical, photocopying, recording or other, without written permission, except by a reviewer who may quote brief passages in a review.

In Honor Of

God

My greatest teacher

My comforter

My friend

CONTENTS

Acknowledgments vii

Preface ix

Introduction 1

Part I: How To Cultivate A Personal Relationship With God 3

Lesson 1: Who Are You God & Why Me? 5

Lesson 2: The First Step Recognize Spirit 17

Lesson 3: Ask For & Expect Spiritual Assistance 29

Lesson 4: From Failure To Refinement 44

Lesson 5: The Road Less Traveled 52

Lesson 6: Love Makes Everything Sacred 64

Lesson 7: Holding The Space 76

Part II: Co-Creation 88

Lesson 8: Your Mind 92

Lesson 9: Your Eyes 107

Lesson 10: Your Mouth 117

Lesson 11: God Never Says No 130

This Is Just The Beginning… 140

ACKNOWLEDGMENTS

I Would like to express my gratitude and love for all the people who have been a part of my life, my family, friends, co-workers and students. I recognize that each of you have served as a teacher along my spiritual journey. Especially the following:

My spiritual mother and mentor, Twyla Michael, who helped me begin to perceive my life in a spiritual manner and set my spiritual journey into motion.

My husband Dee who has always been supportive in allowing me the opportunity to change and grow into the woman that God wants me to become.

My kids, Kenny, Lainey, Charlie and Elle, you have blessed my life in so many ways. Thanks for choosing me to be your mom!

My friend and soul-utionist, Siri, who continues to guide, push and encourage me to continually grow toward and reflect the pure love of Christ.

PREFACE

Let me start off by telling you that I am just your everyday average person. I am a mother of four wonderful kids, a wife, a daughter, and a sister. I was raised in the Catholic Church in a small Midwestern town of 16,000. My profession is that of a high school health teacher. I am not a scholar or an expert on the Bible or an expert in anything for that matter. Like most people, I have always tried to be the best person I could be and do my best to live within the philosophy of my Christian upbringing. I am far, very far, from perfect. What I found as I got older and more confident was that I had all these questions: How do I know that there is really a God? Should I just believe there is one because everyone around me tells me so? If there is a God, how can He allow such terrible things to happen to innocent people? Where was God when I needed Him? Does He really hear my prayers? Maybe you have asked yourself some of these same questions or ones similar to mine. I wish I could tell you that I have all the answers for you, but unfortunately, I do not. However, I was jolted "awake" about 15 years ago by a personal crisis and realized that there truly was something Greater. That crisis was the catalyst of my spiritual adventure, and this Divine Adventure persisted and will continue for the rest of my life. What I have learned so far, I am excited to share with you! I want you to be able to experience God for yourself in a personal way just as I have. Each person's spiritual adventure is uniquely designed for them. However, the tools I share with you will help you navigate the twist and turns of your own supernatural adventure. These tools have served as a springboard to propel me to new levels of spiritual growth and have made a huge difference in my life, and the lives of others that are aware of what I am about to share.

As a teacher, when presenting a new lesson, I would ensure that I get my students' attention, teach the bulk of the lesson, and practice what was learned so that they would understand the lesson. I would always end the lesson with a story to confirm what I taught. We are all on a learning journey through life, so I have decided to use the same approach and layout for this book as I did for my students. These lessons I share have been around since the beginning of time, but many have been discounted and not shared with the masses. Fortunately for me, I had a 72-year-old neighbor named Twyla, who began to mentor and teach me what I am going to share with you.

As you read this book, it is important to remember that some of what is written may seem odd or contradict what you have heard, think, or maybe what your religion taught you. I can assure you that many times when Twyla would teach me something that was not within my belief system, I would think "that's a little nuts" or "I can't believe that is true." Most of us are doubters by nature and that is okay. The most important thing you can do as you read the following pages is to keep an open mind and to hold up to Love what you read for confirmation, so that it resonates within your own soul. Listen to your intuition and not your logical thinking brain. The fascinating thing is - you will be shown. If someone told me 10 years ago some of the things, I know to be true today, I would have thought he/she had lost his/her mind. So, as you read this book, I am giving you permission and inviting you to question what you read, just as I have done and continue to do. You will find that it doesn't matter what you think now or what you have done in your past. The most important thing is to keep an open mind. God will show you the truth.

My goal for you when you read this book is to equip you with simple tools and teach you how to use them for your own spiritual growth- so that you know without a doubt, there really is a God. Not because I will convince you so, but because He will actually show you for yourself through personal experience. KISS, keep it simple stupid, is a tag line I heard often as a kid from my Dad who was a teacher and coach. He always said while teaching someone something new to keep it simple, and they will grasp the material more easily. This is so true, especially when we talk about God and how to have a personal relationship with Him. If you think about it, the world and religion often make God complicated by using all kinds of confusing Bible verses, deep philosophical explanations, rules, regulations and even misrepresenting God for their own personal agendas. All these things can down right intimidate someone from even attempting a spiritual journey to know the Divine, God. I can't tell you how many times I tried to sit down and read the Bible only to be confused and frustrated because of my lack of understanding. I thought I would never be able understand or really know God personally.

Thankfully, Twyla helped me realize that knowing God is simple, and He is that way purposefully so that no one is excluded from knowing him intimately. Twyla is a Christian and often used Bible verses to support what she was teaching me. I will do the same throughout the book. If you do not come from a biblical background, do not let the Bible verses get in the way of reading on. There are valuable learnings in the lessons. My wish for you is that you are able to feel the joy and peace that comes from simply knowing God and that you will use these tools as a spiritual springboard for developing a personal relationship with Him.

INTRODUCTION

Congratulations! It is no accident that you are reading this book. You are being drawn to know God in an intimate way. It makes no difference what religion you are, what background you come from, what "good" or "bad" things you have done, or even if you are unsure about whether there is a God or not. God is eager to teach anyone who is willing to seek Him. *"No one can come to me unless the Father who sent me draws them, and 'I will raise them up on the last day it is written in the Prophets: They will all be taught by God. Everyone who has heard the Father and learned from him comes to me.'* (John 6:44-45, NIV) Most likely something challenging or traumatic has happened in your life, or there is a stirring of your soul for something more that has spurred you to seek. There are probably questions you want answered and doubts you want confirmed. Maybe you have heard accounts of others "awakening" and wondered if what they were saying was true; or wondered why anything hasn't ever happened to "awaken me?" This is your time! God is calling you out of the worldly ways and is ready to take you on an exciting and miraculous adventure. However, you have to be a willing participant. It is your choice; God does not force himself upon anyone. Are you willing to open your mind to new possibilities? Are you willing to walk away from your old ways of acting and thinking that do not serve you? Are you open to being persecuted for the truth you are about to be shown because it doesn't always fall in line with what religions and the world teaches? Are you ready to push forward when resistance comes at you from every possible angle? These questions can seem quite scary. Changes can be scary!

This adventure is not for the faint of heart. It is not easy, and it won't be without times of doubt. However, I can assure you that if you say "yes" to God, it will be the most fascinating, miraculous, and life-altering experience you have ever and will ever have. The seekers journey to know God intimately never ends but will only get better and more exciting every step of the way. Let's begin….

PART I

HOW TO CULTIVATE A PERSONAL RELATIONSHIP WITH GOD

WHAT LIES BEFORE US

AND WHAT LIES BEHIND US

ARE SMALL MATTERS

COMPARED TO

WHAT LIES

WITHIN US

Ralph Waldo Emerson

LESSON 1

WHO ARE YOU GOD & WHY ME?

I use the term God because that is the term I was taught growing up in Catholic schools. This Higher Power, the Creator of All Good Things, can have many different names depending on what religion you were raised in, or the thoughts and beliefs that resonate with you. Here are some of the names that are used to describe this Higher Power: Divine Spirit, Yahweh, Universal Life Force, Om, Father, The Source, God, Brahma, Krishna, Tao, Great Consciousness, and The Great I Am, etc.… It doesn't matter what you call Him, it only matters that you recognize or are open minded enough to the belief that there is or could be a Higher Power.

Quantum physics has proven that there is a Universal Energy that runs through all matter. We have always been able to feel the different energetic frequencies in people. Now science is supporting and in continual study of this energy, and how it affects matter. One of the most interesting things quantum physicists observed in their experiments was that; an observer affects the wave patterns of energy. This in turn is what many "new age" thinkers term the Law of Attraction. Whether you are from a scientific, spiritual, or religious background, quantum physics discoveries point to a higher power source. Many may have trouble comprehending this higher power on an intellectual level. Usually, people tend to be swayed through either scientific reasoning or religious reasoning. What I have come to understand is that there is no separation between scientific and religious reasoning where energy is concerned. They are one and the same. However, you choose to look at the relationship between energy and matter is all up to you and is okay.

The universal energy that quantum physics has proven to be in all matter, I choose to refer to as God. He is the Universal Energy that flows through all of His creation, from the smallest subatomic particle to every person in the universe, including you. The Bible supports this concept, *"don't you know that you yourselves are God's temple and that God's spirit dwells in your midst?"* (1Corinthians 3:16, NIV) And also, *"You, however, are not in the realm of the flesh but are in the realm of the Spirit; if indeed the Spirit of God lives in you."* (Romans 8:9, NIV) Yes, God resides within you. You are a spark off of his divine flame. He is the Creator and energetic source of all things. Most importantly He is pure unconditional love.

So if God is in you, He has always been with you and is with you at this very moment. Jeremiah 1:5 reinforces, *"Before I formed you in the womb, I knew you, before you were born I set you apart."* Now if you have never heard of God or have never had a personal experience with Him, you might be thinking "prove it," like most people. The good news is - God will prove it to you. He has been and continues to pursue you. He is waiting for you to recognize His voice and feel his love and turn to Him. There is nothing God wants more than to have a personal relationship with you. He wants to be the co-creator of your life. More than anything, He desires you to experience his unconditional love first hand. You don't have to prove or do anything to receive His love. He loves you just as you are and is willing to meet you wherever you are. He wants you to know that he is real beyond a shadow of a doubt. You can begin to trust him with all your baggage, hard times, and everyday challenges. God wants to lift your burdens and guide you through the "roller coaster" of life.

Get out of God's Way

God wants to interact with you on a supernatural level. If you don't currently have a supernatural relationship with God, it is because of you. You need to get out of the way, so He can begin to work in your life for your greatest good. If you look at God in the same way you would look at an earthly Father, wouldn't he love his children so much that he would want the best for them? Wouldn't he want to see them reach their potential? Wouldn't he want his kids to have the desires of their hearts? Wouldn't he want them to be happy, free from worry, pain, and suffering? God is your Heavenly Father. He wants all these things and more for you. His love is unconditional. The only thing stopping you from having the desires of your heart and living the life you want is you. You are the one stopping the flow of God's grace and love for yourself.

So often we prevent ourselves from having a personal relationship with God because of fear. Some may think that God has been keeping score and tracking all of our "badness" like Santa. We begin thinking we are way too behind, bad, or not worthy to be near Him. Often, we have the wrong perception of what God is going to ask of us. God doesn't say you have to become a Bible thumper or be perfect. You don't have to stop having fun, stop having a glass of wine or a couple of beers. So, relax, the bigger problem is that we are raised in a culture that teaches us it is weak to ask for help or to be vulnerable. We think we have to have all the answers, and if we don't, we should pretend we do. Society teaches us that we are not good enough; that to be successful or to be liked, you have to be rich, skinny, have the right clothes, have all the right toys, etc. If not, you are a lesser person. Therefore, we end up hiding our true selves and pretending to be someone we are not. God's world is nothing like our society teaches. "*My kingdom is not of this world.*" (John 18:36, NIV) When we focus on the things of the world, we are consumed with trying to fulfill worldly things outside ourselves like money, power, prestige, success, beauty, and possessions all to satisfy the ego. Our ego traps us by making us stay busy in mind and body. When we are so busy, we never pause for the spiritual. We never look for the God energy within us, because the EGO has Edged God Out.

God understands on a human level that trust has to be earned. Therefore, He is willing to help establish your trust in Him one step at a time. He only asks that when He shows you the first step, you take action so that trust and faith in Him can be built up inside you. This can be scary. We want to see the whole plan before we take the first step or take a leap. "Faith is taking the first step even when you can't see the whole staircase." (Martin Luther King) God has been waiting on you to take the first step toward Him. It is your choice. Will you take the first step?

Practice

Take time each day to pause and contemplate what you have read in Lesson 1. Allow yourself to be vulnerable and open minded about Lesson 1. It's ok to say, "I am not sure about all of this, but I am willing to keep an open mind until I am shown."

Keep your ego in check by guarding your mind from the resistance you may be feeling because of preconceived notions of who God is and how He works.

Stories of Confirmation

My First Step

Even though I was raised in a church environment, I did not know God on a personal level or even really knew what that meant or how to achieve it. If there was a God like I was taught, I was pretty sure I was making Him happy, because I was a rules girl. I did what was right most of the time, went to church every Sunday, put on a smile, and took care of myself so as not to bother anyone. I grew up a people pleaser, doing whatever I could do to make everyone happy, even if it was at my own expense. My parents were great, but if my ideas were out of line with theirs, I quickly conformed to their way of thinking. Therefore, I chose a career that my Dad thought was the best for me; I got married at a young age and started having babies because that was what a woman was supposed to do in our family. I was the do-it-all mom and submissive spouse. When things were not so great, I sucked it up, stayed busy, and kept my feelings to myself to keep up the façade that everything was fine. Life was normal, so I thought.

Well, the shoe finally dropped when I was 33. I could no longer pretend I was happy. A great sadness came over me. It was relentless. All that I knew to be normal began to unravel. Like most people, my first reaction was to blame everyone else for my unhappiness. I became angry with my parents, siblings, husband, and my church. I began to rebel like a teenager. No one knew what to do with a rebellious 33-year-old! So, my Dad threatened me to straighten up like I was a teenager. My Mom said, "Maybe everything will be better when you are 50. Hang in there." My Husband just hollered and tried to cage the raging bull.

Fortunately, it didn't take me long to realize that I was destroying my life and hurting my kids with my rebellion. I remember lying in bed one morning feeling completely alone and crying. I thought, "I can't do this anymore. God if you are real, I need your help to get me out of this funk. Just tell me what to do, and I will do it". The crazy thing is; I had spent my whole life trying to be the good girl, do the right thing, and take care of myself. It was when I was at my worst state of mind and actions, when I was ashamed of myself, and when I gave up on trying to control everything, God showed me His unconditional love. He showed up when I least expected. A great peace came over me and I knew that He would help me work everything out. It would all be okay.

That was the first time I felt God's presence in my life, not because He was never there before, but because it was the first time that I took time to pause. It was the first time I turned my life over to a Power Greater than myself, allowed myself to be vulnerable and ask for God's help. It was the first time I stopped avoiding my unhappiness, and trusted that he would work everything out. That moment of surrender was the first step on my spiritual journey with Him. He didn't show me the whole staircase, or swoop right in and fix my life right away. It was a process of my unlearning wrong teachings and replacing my old ways with His new ways. He began to teach me by bringing my neighbor Twyla into my life. Twyla was my first spiritual mentor and was crucial to my knowing

God in a personal way. You'll hear much about her and her teachings throughout this book. My journey began 15 years ago and continues today. It has been and still is the most life transforming, miraculous, joyful and exciting experience ever and is the basis for this book. I wish I hadn't waited until I was 33 to invite Him in, hear His whispers of pursuit, and take the first step. However, we must trust the timing of our process. I know I wasn't ready to give Him control of my life earlier.

"AHA" Moment

I was relieved when my Mom finally passed, so she didn't have to endure anymore suffering from brain cancer. I knew she was in a better place. Although I was sad, I knew she was pain-free. Nine months later the grief hit me hard, and I cried for a week. I was crying because I missed her, but more so because I had been looking forward to developing a closer relationship with her after her retirement. Our relationship had always been somewhat distant; I was looking forward to getting close to her. I had dreams of spending time with her, traveling, and just hanging out together once she retired.

My Mom was a hard worker, the Mother of four kids, and 18 grandchildren. If she was not working, she was usually helping out my older sister who was trying to raise seven kids alone. Because Mom was often exhausted, I would never bother her with any of my problems, ask her to babysit my kids, or ask her to come to their sporting events. I would often get my feelings hurt because it seemed she was more interested in my siblings and their kids than me and my family. I always thought that she loved my other siblings more than me, and I had some resentment toward her for not outwardly giving me the love I so much wanted from her.

Three years after her death, even though I loved and appreciated her, I still was unable to let go of the hurt I felt when I thought of my Mom. I knew that she had been a good Mom; I tried to forget the hurt, but it kept popping back up. I prayed for help in healing my hurt, since I clearly couldn't do it on my own. Shortly after, I joined a bible study group. During the study of the "prodigal son," God revealed to me an important lesson that healed my hurt.

My Mom had always been there for me but, I never asked, or acted like I needed her. My desire to not be a burden to her, and to be independent, kept me from a close relationship with her. My siblings all relied on her in some way, and she always helped them. My Mom wasn't the problem, I was. What an AHA moment! God reminded me, that you have to be willing to have help with your life, and to ask for what you need. It is the same with Him. He is always there for us, but until we turn to Him, and ask, He can't complete all the wonderful plans He has for our lives.

Bill is a Blessing & is Blessed

Bill was in the hospital waiting room, bent over sobbing after getting the news that his wife of 30 years had stage four colon cancer and had only days to live. As he straightened up, he noticed a teenage girl and boy looking at him. After he collected himself, he went back into his wife's room to be with the family. His daughter, Sara asked where his iPhone 5 was, so he walked back to the waiting room to look on the chair where he had left it. No phone, "great he thought. Could this day get any worse- $350 bucks gone?" He immediately knew that the teens had taken his phone. When Sara heard this, she opened her laptop and tracked his phone. It was about 2 blocks from the hospital. She dialed the number and a boy answered saying he had just bought the phone for $75. Sara explained that it was Bill's phone, and he would like it back. The kid agreed to bring it back to the hospital if he could get his $75 bucks back.

In the meantime, the nursing staff had phoned security and they went to the main hospital entrance to await the exchange and to arrest the boy if Bill told them it was the same boy in the waiting room. Bill made his way to the ATM to get the $75. As he stood in front of the ATM, he felt a strong intuition to take out $100 instead. He was so angry and couldn't believe it. All he wanted to do was snap the kid in half, but God was telling him to take out $100 and give it to the punk who stole his phone. On the worst day of his life he was being asked to do God's work. He got the $100 and headed angrily to the main lobby. When the boy walked in with the phone, Bill recognized him from the waiting room. Security started to move forward to arrest the boy, but Bill held them off. He walked up to the boy nose-to-nose and handed the boy the $100. Bill said, "What you deserve is jail; what you are getting is a gift. This is the good news of the Gospel. What we deserve is hell but what God offers is eternal life. God loves you." The boy began to cry. He told Bill his mom was upstairs dying of cancer. Bill walked with the boy up to his mother's room, and he prayed with them. He recognized in his most heartbreaking trial that God was showing him His love by supplying him with the grace and knowledge to speak God's gospel to a lost soul. It also reminded him that in all things, God is in control, and although we might not understand His ways, He has a greater plan. Thankfully, Bill listened and followed through with what God called him to do. It was time to turn the young man around. God sure got his attention!

Why wait for God to do something drastic in your life to get your attention? Begin today to seek Him. It will be the best decision you ever make. Take the first step....

A mother and her 3 toddlers were driving home from Grandma's house. What fun they were having blaring the radio and singing at the top of their lungs as they approached the railroad tracks. The mother's view of the north track was blocked by a building and huge rock pile. No worries. The crossing gate was up and no lights were flashing. Just before entering the crossing, she had an intuition to look north. She slammed on the brakes as the engine hurled a foot in front of the car. She knows they all should have died that day, but thankfully, Spirit intervened!

LESSON 2

THE FIRST STEP RECOGNIZE SPIRIT

It is important that you begin to perceive that we live in a spiritual world where Spirit is in us and all around us. You are already aware of this; you may have never given it much thought or paid much attention to it. Have you ever suddenly thought of someone you haven't seen in a while, and then later ran into them, or got a call from them? That is Spirit. Have you ever had a strong gut feeling or strong intuition about something? That is Spirit. Have you ever had a stroke of creative genius or done something so out of the ordinary like it was second nature? That is Spirit. Have you ever had a strong emotional reaction, which seemed to have no source? That is Spirit. Have you seen an apparition, or had an imaginary friend when you were little? That is Spirit. You are more spiritually aware than you know or give yourself credit for.

We are all spiritual beings. Religion refers to spirit as light, or soul. "*You are the light of the world. A town built on a hill cannot be hidden.*" (Matt 5:14, NIV) Science refers to it as energy. Dr. Robert Fulford, D.O., states in his book <u>Touch of Life,</u> "It is my firm belief, after more than a half century of reading, debating, questioning, and contemplating, that the human body is surrounded by something that I call a life field…. This life field conveys vitality to your physical body and provides you with your spirit." We all have a spirit residing in each of us. It is this Spiritual Energy, which is the driving force behind all human and universal laws.

Our spirit is the direct link to God and is affected by the universal energy that is in all creation. This spirit lives on after our bodies have worn out. Thanks to the media and science, it is easier for most of us to wrap our head around the idea of spirit and the spiritual world we live in. Due to current television programing we can watch shows about ghosts, paranormal activity, near death and out of body experiences. There are also shows about psychics and mediums. With the advances of technology, science is now able to back up the spiritual phenomenon. Your spirit has always been a part of you. Just as science has proven that there is a natural evolution in life, there is also an evolution of spirit.

Spiritual evolution involves being intimate with the presence of God, that is already within you. All His knowing and wisdom is within you. Your job is to seek Him from within. This is why many spiritual teachers agree that man's greatest journey is ever with himself, through the process of spiritual evolution. *"I love those who love me, and those who seek me find me."* (Proverbs 8:17, NIV), *"Seek the Lord and his strength, seek his face continually."* (1Chronicles 16:11, NIV) When we begin to seek Him, you begin your own unique evolutionary journey. A journey to awaken to something more and to live into your souls' purpose.

One of the first lessons Twyla taught me was to start paying attention to Spirit. She reminded me, that Spirit was in me- the all-knowing, divine presence of God. Also, Spirit was all around me in all of God's creations. Spirit was to be utilized as a tool, to help one navigate life from the smallest to the largest needs. She explained, most people don't consider asking for help from the spiritual beings like angels, guides, and God, who are always available to us. Most also don't look within their own spirit for answers, and solutions to the things going on in their lives. Twyla gave me a simple exercise to help me build trust in God. She said, "The next time you are cooking and struggling to open a jar, just pause and ask for help to open it." This was a practice of blind faith. "You have to believe you will receive help opening the jar, without any doubt" she said. *"But when you ask, you must believe and not doubt, because the one who doubts is like a wave of the sea, blown and tossed by the wind. That person should not expect to receive anything from the Lord."* (James 1:6-7, NIV) At the moment of our birth, God equips us with a team of spiritual beings to help us. We have to be willing to ask for help and listen to our intuition. *"For he will command his angels concerning you to guard you in all your ways."* (Psalm 91:11, NIV) *"Are not all angels ministering spirits sent to serve those who will inherit salvation?"* (Hebrews 1:14, NIV) You have all the help you need, surrounding you all the time, by divine design.

I would be lying if I said that Twyla's exercise worked for me the first time, and even the second. However, when I finally opened my mind up to the possibility, and quieted my doubting mind, spirit stepped in. The top of the jar popped off with ease. I had to get to a place where I was not forcing the outcome and just letting Spirit flow through me. This exercise is now part of my daily practice. I have used it to find lost objects, remember people's names, start a stalled car, and to assist others in need. God, his angels, and your spiritual guides, are willing to help with these little things. How much more could they help you with? The possibilities are endless! Not only has this practice helped relieve stress, but it has brought so much comfort to me, knowing God wants to, and is willing to be part of my daily life. He is an everyday God!

Get out of God's Way

Now that we have established that there is a Spirit, also know that every living thing created is from God and has His Spirit in it. We are born with the capability to be in the flow of His Spirit. Often, we get in the way of what God wants to do in our lives and get in the way of receiving help from Spirit. Let's take a look at how we can hinder God's work in our lives:

1. Not asking for assistance. We have to allow ourselves to be vulnerable. In her book <u>Daring Greatly</u>, Brene Brown states "Vulnerability does not know victory or defeat, its understanding the necessity of both; it's engaging." It's being all in. This is where transformation of spirit begins. Recognizing we can't do it all alone and asking for God's help.

2. Doubting. We have grown up hearing the phrase "I can't never could do anything" So it is with God. You don't have to understand how it is all going to work, just believe. Doubting stops the Flow of Spirit.

3. Trying to force the outcome. Every time I would grab the lid and twist as hard as I could, the darn thing would not open. When I would relax into Spirit, and twist with ease, Voila, open jar. It's about relaxing and pausing so that the angels can assist you.

4. Not listening to your intuition. Your intuition is tied directly to Spirit. When you don't listen to it, you are

ignoring God. You are missing out on things God wants to help you with, protect you from, or bless another through you.

5. Not pausing to notice or acknowledge Spirit at work. Sometimes we become so busy, we don't pause long enough to see God at work in our lives or how God is using us to benefit others. In our own lives we might say that we got lucky or that it was just a coincidence. No, that is Spirit at work! Slow down, God is in the pauses of life.

6. Forgetting to be grateful. When we have a grateful heart, God can work in our lives more easily. Forgetting to say thanks when Spirit has helped you in any way blocks the flow of more help coming your way. The small stuff really does matter. Be grateful in small things and God then blesses you in larger ways. *"Rejoice always, pray continually, and give thanks in all circumstances; for this is God's will for you in Christ Jesus."* (1 Thessalonian 5:16, NIV)

Practice

Go outside or look out of the window. Pick a cloud in the sky. I would choose the one that is not huge, for time's sake. As you look at the cloud, simply say to yourself, "Please help me make that cloud disappear." Now, just watch the cloud. If doubting thoughts come in to your mind, just repeat the phrase above. Slowly, you will see the cloud begin to break up and disappear before your eyes. It is amazing! God wants you to know that He is with you, and that his helping hand is boundless.

Ask for help with other simple things like finding lost objects, remembering something, etc. Practice helps to open the flow of Spirit in the doubting mind. Don't forget to say thank you as Spirit works to help you!

Listen to your intuition, and then take action. Your intuition tries to guide you, but you have free-will choice as to whether to listen and take action on it or not. *"In the same way, faith by itself, if it is not accompanied by action, is dead."* (James 2:17, NIV) You must take action.

Stories of Confirmation

Grandpa's Spiritual Visit

My uncle called the house one day to inform everyone that grandpa was in the hospital. He had a mild heart attack. My parents made the 2-hour drive immediately. Later, they phoned to say that grandpa was doing fine, but would stay in the hospital for a few days for observation. I remember thinking, I would give grandpa a call instead of loading up my toddlers and making the drive. I would let my husband stay with the kids while I went to visit grandpa over the weekend. I called grandpa's hospital room and he answered the phone. I said, "Hi grandpa, I am calling to check on you, and I will be up on Saturday to visit." He said, "Who is this?" "It's Pammy" I said. Grandpa's hearing was not too good, and I could tell from the rest of the conversation that he was just being polite and had no idea who he was talking to. I told him bye and that I loved him and hung up the phone believing I would see him on Saturday. Two days later, he had another heart attack and died. I remember feeling so guilty because I didn't make the trip to see him. I told my dad that I had called, and he didn't know who I was.

Apparently, he told some family members who tried to make me feel better at the funeral. They claimed grandpa knew I had called. I knew in my heart what they were saying was not true.

The first week went by after his death, and every time I thought of him waves of guilt swept through me. About 10 days after his death, I had a very vivid dream about my grandpa. He was standing beside my bed and he told me that he knew I called to check on him, and he told me he loved me. When I woke up in the morning, I remembered the dream, and the guilt I had been carrying was gone. I know for certain that grandpa's spirit stopped by for a visit, to release me of my guilt. Spirit lives on after physical death.

God Sends Lea

A friend of mine named Lea, who is kind of a tomboy, stopped by an office at work one day to ask the woman who worked in there a question. When she entered the office, the woman was on the phone. Lea decided to stay there and wait until she hung up because the woman had signaled the "just a minute" sign to her. As Lea stood there, she had a thought pop into her head about how pretty the woman's hair looked. Since Lea was a tomboy, she usually didn't notice stuff like that, and never commented on how someone was dressed, or about their hair. When the woman hung up the phone, Lea got her question answered and was about ready to walk out the door, when she thought about the woman's hair again. As an afterthought, she finally spoke up and said to the woman, "Your hair really looks pretty today." The woman immediately broke down sobbing. Lea thought she did something wrong, until the woman spoke up. She said, "You don't know how much that means to me. This is actually a wig and it is the first day I have ever worn it. I have been going through chemo and my hair was so bad I couldn't hide it any longer. I was so worried about wearing this wig, thank you for saying something." Thankfully, Lea listened to Spirit; she was a blessing to the woman, who was going through a difficult time. God knew she needed to feel His touch. I am sure many other people went to her office that same day and noticed her hair but chose not to listen to Spirit. Follow your intuition and watch how God will work through you and for you.

A Teacher's Blessing

I was doing a maternity leave in Biology at the local high school before I was hired on full time. I usually don't have many problems in my classroom, I treat the kids with respect and in turn that respect is shown back to me. However, there was one particular hour where there was a student named Josh who was determined to be the class goof and test my patience. It was pretty clear that he had no interest in Biology, or in school, other than socializing. I didn't see Josh as a bad kid, but rather as a student who wasn't in the right mind set. Over the next couple of weeks, I did what any teacher would do to get him to conform to the rules so that he would not be a disruption to other students learning. I moved his seat to the front, stood by his desk during class, tried to engage him in learning, kindly talked to him after class about his behavior, called home, and finally as the last resort, sent him to the office. Josh would go to in school supervision for a day or two and come right back to class with the same behavior. I was getting pretty frustrated when it dawned on me to try

Twyla's approach about asking for help from above. I put it out there "If Josh is to stay in my class to learn something from me or I am to learn something from him then please transform his behavior. If not, please have him removed from my class." I wasn't sure if this was going to work, but it was worth a try. I started saying this on Tuesday and turned all my doubts over to God and waited. When he came to class on Wednesday, he was tired from staying up all night, so wasn't such a problem. Josh didn't come to school on Thursday or Friday, which wasn't unusual since he missed a lot of school. When he returned on Monday, he informed the class that it was his last day, because his family was moving. Upon questioning, I found out that the move was sudden and unplanned. I gave Josh some words of encouragement and wished him well. Then I thanked Spirit for helping out! Over the course of my eight years of teaching, I have used this several times. The interesting thing is, most of the time, the students will transform before my very eyes and often go from being a pain, to one of my favorite students. Josh was the only one who ever moved. However, I have had students' schedules changed unexpectedly, taking them out of my class. God doesn't want to see you stressed out; He helps if you ask and believe.

Supernatural Healing

My daughter Lainey loved playing volleyball as an outside hitter on the high school team. During her junior year she began to have problems with her collarbone dislocating when she spiked the ball. The dislocation would cause her much pain and interfered with her play. We took her to an orthopedic doctor and were told that her collarbone was too short. The force of her arm swing against the force of the ball was enough to dislocate it. The doctor had said there was nothing that could be done. She would have to stop playing or live with the pain. She chose to play the rest of the season and we had a chiropractor pop it back in place many times. Around the same time, a new spiritual teacher had come into my life that was very far along in her spiritual journey and had many gifts, one being that of a healer. One day when I was complaining about how much money we were spending at the chiropractor to fix her dislocations, she told me to bring Lainey by her house after practice. That evening, I took Lainey over to her house and she asked Lainey if she could pray over her collarbone. Lainey agreed, so she placed her hand over Lainey's collarbone and prayed in Jesus name. Lainey said she felt a pulsing sensation coming from the healer's hands as she prayed. Interestingly, from then on Lainey played the rest of her volleyball season with her collarbone never dislocated again! She played her entire senior season injury free, and to this day, Lainey has never had trouble again. God allowed His healing spirit to flow through my teacher to Lainey, she was healed in an instant. Sometimes God's spirit moves fast and furious, and sometimes slow and steady. However, we must ask, and believe before we can receive.

The old king said, "Never Stop Dreaming. When you want something, the whole universe conspires to help you achieve it. In order to find the treasure, you will have to follow the omens. God has prepared a path for everyone to follow. You just have to read the omens that he has left for you."

– The Alchemist, Paulo Coelho

LESSON 3

ASK FOR & EXPECT SPIRITUAL ASSISTANCE

This lesson is so exciting for me, because you are about to witness God perform miracles in your life! God is a supernatural Being and His miracles are recorded all throughout the Old and New Testaments in the Bible. Google™ God's miracles and you will see all of them listed from miracles involving nature, healings of sicknesses, driving out demons, raising people from the dead, parting the Red Sea, and something as unimportant as helping out at a wedding by turning water into wine. He is the same God today as He was way back then, and He continues to be supernatural and bestow miracles upon His believers. Webster's dictionary defines miracle as, "an unusual or wonderful event that is believed to be caused by the power of God." Miracles serve as evidence of God, they can increase faith, be used as confirmation of a message from God, fulfill the needs of people, and they always show God's glory. No matter why you would like to see a miracle in your life, God is willing to be your supernatural God too.

When Twyla first explained this lesson to me, I needed to know that the loving God she taught me about, and the one who was helping me open jars was willing to interact with little, unworthy, me on a supernatural level. I needed to know that He heard me and was willing to help me transform my life to something greater; He was willing to guide me in the right direction. At this particular time, I was going through a personal struggle and a woman allowed me to ride her horse. When I was feeling overwhelmed, I would go to her barn and saddle up. That led me to going to an auction because there were saddles listed in the sale advertisement. While I was at the auction, I ran into my best friend's Dad from high school. I hadn't seen him in years. While talking with him, he asked if I was ever going to move to the country, so I could have a horse of my own. I said, "Maybe someday." He then turned to the lady beside him, introduced us and said, "She just happens to own a house in the country that she hasn't put on the market." She had never listed the property because someone wanted to put a strip club on it. The property has been in her family for 100 years, and she was not willing to let that happen, so it has sat vacant for 7 years. I told her I would take a look at it and call her if I was interested. This was very stressful to me, because I loved my big old house. It had character, enough room for a family of six, my mom and dad lived two doors down, and my spiritual mentor lived next door. On top of all of that, the other house was a very old, rundown farmhouse with only two bedrooms and one tiny bathroom. It was also priced way above anything we could afford, because it sat on 60 acres. However, the circumstances surrounding how the farm house even came into play made me have an intuition that this was happening for a reason. Maybe we were to move there? When I told my husband about the farmhouse, we took a ride to see it. He thought I was crazy after seeing its dilapidated condition and hearing the price the owner was asking for it. I wasn't sure if I should pursue the farmhouse because of my hubby's negative comments. So, I went to talk it over with Twyla.

Twyla said, "why don't you ask God for a sign?" I wasn't sure what she meant. She explained that God would give me a sign about the farmhouse, if I just asked. She said that God was always willing to help guide us through life, if we only ask. Twyla then explained it was important that when you ask for a sign, you believe you will receive it. She also said, "The sign will be so out of the ordinary that you will recognize God in it." Isaiah 7:11, says *"Ask the Lord your God for a sign, whether in the deepest depths or in the highest heights."* So as Twyla suggested I asked for a sign saying, "If our family is to move to the farmhouse, then please show me a sign of confirmation." The following day it was a beautiful sunny day. I decided to jump into the car and take a drive out past the farmhouse. As I slowed down in the road and looked at the house, shooting out of the roof was a beautiful rainbow that covered the whole property. I looked at the sky and there was not a cloud in it. I knew without a doubt that the rainbow was a miracle, and my sign. This was not the first miracle God showed me, but it was the first miracle I recognized. I was too spiritually asleep to ask for, or to recognize God's guidance in previous ones.

If you have been raised in church, the concept of asking for a sign might throw up a red flag for you. Some churches teach that asking for a sign is testing God, or that it is evil, because the following Bible verse is taken out of context. *"Then some of the Pharisees and teachers of the law said to him, Teacher, we want to see a sign from you. He answered, a wicked and adulterous generation asks for a sign. But none will be given it except the sign of the prophet Jonah."* (Matthew 12:38-39, NIV) In this verse, the Pharisees and teachers (religious leaders) had already seen many signs and miracles that Jesus had performed. Their hearts were hardened, they had turned to their own man-made rules and demanded something more than all the miracles they had already witnessed. Jesus knew nothing would make them believe, and therefore called them evil and adulterous. *"In spite of all this, they kept on sinning; in spite of his wonders, they did not believe."* (Psalms 78:32, NIV) God is willing to give signs to his believers; to build trust, faith, and to give direction. He knows that the nature of the human spirit is to doubt. *"Unless you see signs and wonders you will not believe."* (John 2:23, NIV) Therefore, don't be afraid, or think it is wrong of you to ask for a sign. He knows your heart, your intentions, and as long as you are sincerely seeking him, a sign will be given unto you. Let Him be your supernatural God, ask for a sign!

On my spiritual journey, I have learned from other mentors' specific steps to take when asking for a sign which makes the process a lot easier. Here are the steps to the confirmation prayer.

1. Be specific with your question

2. Ask; if it is His will for your life? If you are making choices that are in line with His will for your life, then life is smooth. So, when appropriate, I always ask for His will to be done. However, sometimes that statement might not apply. Sometimes I just ask for a sign that things are going to be OK when I am stressed out. Other times, to have the comfort that He is working things out.

3. Choose what kind of sign you want to see. When choosing a sign, it is important that you don't use people. People make their own choices, and sometimes they feel that they should do something, but they don't always do it. You don't want to rely on them being able to hear God, and to take action. I like to use nature, because God reigns over it. You can also use sounds, songs, colors, and numbers, just anything without a thinking mind.

4. Put a time limit on it. Without a time, limit, the urgency isn't there. Your sign might not show itself for a while, and this can be confusing.

5. Be thankful and believe you will receive it. *"Because you have seen me, you have believed; blessed are those who have not seen and yet have believed."* (John 20:29, NIV)

6. Always say thank you after the time limit is up even if you didn't get a sign or get the one you were hoping for.

Asking for a sign is pretty easy, lets practice with an example. Let's say you have been offered a new job and you want confirmation as to whether you should take it. Your statement would be something like this: "Father, if it is your will that I should take the new job offer, please have a hawk circle over me on my drive home today. In Jesus name, I thank you." Adding "in Jesus name," is important, *"And I will do whatever you ask in my name, so that the Father may be glorified in the Son. You may ask for anything in my name, and I will do it."* (John 14:13-14, NIV) If a hawk circles you on the way home, you know that you are to take the job. However, sometimes God does not give you a sign. He is leaving the choice up to you. So, if I didn't get a sign, I might then ask, "If you are leaving the choice to me please confirm that you will bless my choice by showing me the number 555 before I go to bed tonight." If you see the number 555, then He is saying the choice is yours and His will for you will be done at either job. If you don't see the number 555, that would mean to stay at your current job. It is a great way to allow God the opportunity to guide you in His will for your life. Asking for a sign through a confirmation prayer also helps to relieve unnecessary worry and stress.

Get out of God's Way

Sometimes, you can get in the way of God's supernatural miracles by having a closed mind or not asking for a sign. He can't work with you if you don't ask. Once God shows you a sign, it is important to guard your mind against disbelief or thoughts that contradict the sign you were given. That is testing God. When He shows you signs and direction, but you continually go the other way out of His will for your life, struggles will come from ignoring Him. He will stand back awhile and allow you to experience the consequences of your choices. This is not to be mean, but to help you learn to trust and have faith in His direction for your life. Seeking Him only in bad times for your rescue and dropping Him during good times is using God. Doing so will often lead to feeling like God is apart from you. God will stand back until you understand that he wants a relationship with you all the time, good and bad. God knows your heart and motives for asking, so make sure they are in the right place. You can also get in the way by relying too heavily on signs, rather than in trusting God, and having faith in Him. Signs are to be used as comfort, to build faith, to show love, and to give direction for the bigger things in life.

At first, when signs started showing up for me, I had feelings of unworthiness. September 11th had just occurred, and there I was asking for help with my little problems. I knew my problems were small in comparison to what had happened in New York and the ongoing terror around the world. Yet he was still there for me. I learned that God doesn't rank or compare our problems with someone else's. He is big enough, patient enough, and loving enough to answer a cry of help from any of his children who reach out to Him. When God began to teach me about signs, I became so excited that my doubts faded away. I was truly amazed at the miracles and the work God was doing in my life. "*Did I not tell you that if you believe, you will see the glory of God?*" (John 11:40, NIV) Oh, how I saw the glory of God.

Above all, be thankful when God steps in to work with you supernaturally. Being ungrateful stops the flow of miracles in your life. "*Give praise to the Lord, proclaim his name; make known among the nations what he has done.*" (Psalms 105:1, NIV) I was so thankful, and I began to share Twyla's lessons with those closest to me. I wanted them to experience the goodness and glory of God for themselves.

Practice

Expect miracles. God was supernatural in the past and He is the same supernatural God today. "*He will teach us his ways, so we can walk in his paths.*" (Micah 4:2, NIV) Ask for a sign. You might want to start with something easy at first to build your faith and confidence in the process. Ask if there really is a God; or ask to know if God hears you or loves you. Just watch what happens.

Ask for a sign of confirmation for something you would like direction or guidance for in your life.

As you begin to ask and receive signs from God, your faith in him will grow. With increased faith, God can teach and expand your knowledge of Him to serve as a place of comfort and peace during all the seasons of your life.

Stories of Confirmation

The Farmhouse

After I saw the rainbow and knew that the house was for us, I had to step out in faith by telling my husband and pressuring him a little to consider the possibility of a move. He agreed to walk the property with me one Saturday morning. As we walked through the wooded trails, we came to the top of a hill and a beautiful pond stood before us surrounded by trees. It was breathtaking, and I could tell my husband was pretty moved by it. That was all it took for him to consider the idea of moving. Being an accountant, he went home to "crunch" the numbers, only to come to the conclusion that there was no way we could come close to the asking price. When we told the seller we couldn't afford it, to our surprise she said, "Shoot me an offer of what you can afford." We were pretty hesitant to do so because it was nearly $50,000 less than the property was worth. That night my husband couldn't sleep, worrying about if he should give her the low-ball offer. He got up and asked God to show him a sign if he should follow through with the offer. As he finished the thought, he stepped into the dark hallway and the light mysteriously came on. He knew that was his sign. We made the low offer and the owner was nice, but said, "I am sorry, I don't believe I can go that low." We thanked her and were disappointed, but fortunately for us, God had other plans. The following day, the owner called us and told us that in the night, she had a very vivid dream telling her to sell us the property at whatever we could afford. She said that she knew it was a sign from above, so she willingly sold the property to us way below market value. Thankfully, the owner and my husband took action as God had shown them to. What a blessing for our family!

The Enchanted Flower

My Mom had been going through a difficult time, her parents moved to town and she helped to care for both of them as they aged, became ill, and died about a year apart. At the same time, my Dad was battling prostate cancer and couldn't work. She was the sole financial support, and on top of that, my sister's family was having problems as well, which added to her stress levels. One day, my mom stopped by my house and my hydrangea bush was in full bloom. That was one of her favorite flowers, so she picked a great big bloom and took it home. I stopped by the following week and noticed the flower in a vase. It looked the same as the day she picked it. Another two weeks past and still the flower had not changed. Three weeks turned into a month and then two months. By this time, everyone was pretty astonished at the flowers longevity. My Mom said, "I don't know what is going on, all I do is keep adding water when the vase is almost empty." After about two and a half months with the flower looking the exact same as the day she picked it, I finally said, "If that isn't a sign from God, I don't know what is." My Mom thought about it and remembered that she had asked God for encouragement to help her through the difficult time in her life. She felt it was the reason why the flower remained alive for so long. The funny thing was that once she recognized Spirit was sending encouragement for her through the flower, it then began to wilt like a normal flower would.

Even though my mom didn't ask for a specific sign, one was still delivered to her because she asked.

Nothing is impossible

I think about spiritual things a lot when I drive. One rainy morning, I had an hour's drive, so I began to ask for confirmation about a challenge I was having with a co-worker. As I was thinking up what kind of sign I wanted to see, a bunch of thoughts ran through my head. I usually like to use a hawk for my sign, but I doubted there would be any out because of the storm. I thought, "How about showing me something funny before I arrive at my destination." Then my next thought, "There is nothing funny that can happen driving down a highway in a thunderstorm." Finally, I thought, "How about showing me an animal of any kind in my path, but nothing to make me wreck." Basically, I went from a bird to something funny, then to an animal in front of my car. As I drove in the pouring rain, I got lost in the music of the radio and forgot about my prayer. All of a sudden, a huge black bird came out of nowhere, swooping toward the hood of my car. It looked me right in the eye through the wind shield, flew over the top and was gone. My initial reaction was that I was startled, but then the birds face made me laugh out loud. It reminded me of something out of a cartoon. As I sat there laughing a bit, it dawned on me that God had not just given me my sign, but He had combined all my thoughts together, to show me that He could deliver a bird in a thunderstorm, in the path of my car, and make me laugh as well! Nothing is impossible with God. He is good, what a confirmation.

Kristy's Cardinal

My niece Kristy stopped by for a visit while she was in town. She had recently started a new job. One that she really didn't want, but her boyfriend of six years, had convinced her to take it. He would move to the same town and eventually marry her. A month into her job, he decided that he was no longer moving and that he was breaking up with her. Of course, she was devastated. She was working a job she didn't want and living in a town that held too many memories of their relationship. She was at a major turning point in her life and was trying to decide what she should do besides cry all the time. I told her about asking for a sign. She had never heard of it before and I could tell she was a little skeptical to try it. When she got home, she decided to give it a try and ask for a sign. Kristy asked to see blue jays if she was supposed to stay where she was and continue with her job. She asked to see cardinals if she should move and quit her job. She really wanted to see those cardinals. When she saw her first blue jay she was bummed. She kept seeing blue jays everywhere for the next couple of months and never once saw a cardinal. A week before she was supposed to renew her job contract for the next school year, she saw a cardinal. She got excited but wondered if that was her sign to move after all this time. So in doubt, she asked to see more cardinals if she should move. The next few days she didn't see any cardinals and became discouraged, thinking that she would probably sign the contract for another year on Monday. That weekend she decided to go to her dad's house for a visit. When she walked into the door to surprise him, he said, "It's so good you are here, I bought you something the other day. When I walked into the store it caught my eye and I immediately thought of you. I picked it up and put it down, but as I walked around the store, I just felt I was to buy it for you." He walked to the other room to get what he bought for her and returned with a stuffed, sequin cardinal pillow. She thought it was the most hideous thing she ever saw, but immediately knew that God had delivered a really big sign. Even though Kristy had an image of a real bird in her mind, God delivered an even more unbelievable cardinal in an unusual manner to really get her attention.

Spiritual Vitamins

I have a good friend named Amare. She is very gifted spiritually and can hear God's direction really well. A few years back, she heard that she was to move to Vermont but wasn't told when. Amare was a California girl and had no desire to move where it was cold or so far away from home. Her family was in California and she was successful in her career there. She waited on God to be clear on the timing of when her move was to happen. About a year after she heard God's directions to move to Vermont, Amare really started to feel a nudge that the time was now. However, she still doubted God's instructions. She kept hearing God repeating that he wanted her to move to Vermont and finally she asked Him, "Father if it is your will that I should move to Vermont, please give me a direct lead and I will go." She began to ask where in Vermont He wanted her to go. Amare heard three places: Bristol, Brattleboro, and Bennington. She prayed and prayed about which town he wanted her to go to, but she could not hear the answer because her heightened emotions of such a big move were getting in the way. One day, lying on her bed, crying in confusion, she said, "I am having trouble hearing where you want me to go, please give me a clear sign, so I can get on with this move." As Amare wiped her eyes and lay back on her pillow, she reached to her nightstand and grabbed the bottle of vitamins she takes every night before bed. She began to read the vitamin label, and was amazed at what she saw, "made in Brattleboro, VT!" These were the same vitamins she had taken for years. What made her decide to read the label that day, for the first time ever? It was definitely Spirit. Her frustration ended, she made plans, and two weeks later, Amare made the cross-country drive to Brattleboro, VT to follow spirit.

"Failure should be our teacher, not our undertaker. Failure is delay, not defeat. It is a temporary detour, not a dead end. Failure is something we can avoid only by saying nothing, doing nothing, and being nothing."

– Denis Waitley

LESSON 4

FROM FAILURE TO REFINEMENT

In our society, failure is a dirty word and viewed negatively. In reality, failure is often a turning point and a defining moment in life. Anyone who is successful at anything knows that success only came because of the lessons learned through previous failures. Failure spurs us to change. Legendary coach John Woodend's quote on failure puts it into perspective, "Failure isn't fatal, but failure to change might be."

I was failing horribly when I first turned my life and everything in it over to God. I was relieved that I was going to have the help I needed and thought I would be on to better days. Boy was I wrong! After saying yes and accepting a relationship with Him, everything in my life actually got worse. Resistance hit me from every angle, trying to get me to turn away from God. Luckily, I placed my hope in Him largely because of the trust that he had been building in me through Twyla's lessons. Looking back, I realized that God was allowing the consequences of my previous actions and failures to refine me. I kept pressing on and seeking Him. Daily, I would make a point to lean on Him and asked Him for help wherever I needed it. He was drawing me in closer and helping me to see where I needed to make changes in my life. Even though things got worse, I knew that He was beside me every minute of every day, helping me to make the refining process easier. This refining period allowed me to shake off my old self and put on the new me, which was more in line with what God's plan was for my life. It was a slow process of refinement, but that was what I needed.

God allows bad things to happen to good and sometimes innocent people for a reason. Sometimes our own or the choices of others, often lead to undesirable consequences, but God always tries to send spirit to us, to warn us about where ours or anothers choices are creating negative consequences, which we might have to deal with. If we do not take notice of Spirit's warnings and make changes, then God allows the consequences. Although we might not understand or like the consequences we have to go through, there is always a learning experience for us in it that ends up drawing us even closer to Him. Even if we think of the most terrible circumstances of something, like the Sandy Hook school shooting. God allows free will choice and the consequences of those choices without interference. God never wants anything bad to happen to anyone and especially innocent children. It was the choice and consequence of the gun man that brought evil. However, God has used that terrible incident to further his Kingdom of Love. There was such an outpouring of love and support for the victims and their families from around the globe. One of the victim's mother travelled to schools around the nation and promoted school safety; and more people were trained to identify those who need mental health intervention. So much good has come from an evil act of another. Love always supersedes evil.

Sometimes, like with me, God has to do something drastic to get our attention. He has always been in pursuit of us, but if we ignore Him, and don't turn around, He allows us to go through a hardship or failure of some sort because our actions have opened the door for them to occur. I ignored the warning signs to make changes, so he allowed me to have the personal crisis I did, brought on by my choices. It is often said, "God never gives you more than you can handle," this is in part true, He allows for a pretty heavy burden, hoping you will turn to Him so that together you can handle it. Most of us are stubborn by nature. We don't always turn to God unless we are desperate and hopeless. When we do turn to Him, we recognize that God wants to be a part of our lives every day and in every way. When we are stubborn and don't turn to God, that burden may end up being too heavy. When a burden is too heavy for an individual, they often resort to drugs, alcohol, suicide or other vices to deal with it.

One thing is certain; we are all going to have trials and failures in this life, either because of our own choices or those of others. The trials and failures serve to refine us and prepare us for what God has in store for us down the road. Romans 5:3-5, gives insight about how to handle trials, *"not only so, but we also glory in our sufferings, because we know that suffering produces perseverance; perseverance, character; and character, hope. And hope does not put us to shame, because God's love has been poured out into our hearts through the Holy Spirit, who has been given to us."* When you begin to look at your trials in a spiritual sense, you are likely to learn your lessons more quickly. You don't have to repeat them, and you handle trials more easily, knowing that God is going to use it for your greatest good. Viewing your trial from a spiritual perspective allows you to move from the place of being a victim of circumstance, to the position of responsibility and helps you to see the big picture and how you can transform it with God's help. "When you think everything is someone else's fault, you will suffer a lot. When you realize that everything springs from yourself, you will learn both peace and joy." (Dalai Lama)

Get out of God's Way

Pete Wilson writes in <u>Let Hope</u> In, "It is not the failure that makes you unusable. It is the unwillingness to move forward and be open to correction. Allow yourself to be usable by allowing forward movement and correction." When things are not going our way, it is easy to play the victim and make excuses. When we play the victim role, we don't stop to consider what lesson we need to learn from the situation at hand. We have a tendency to blame others instead of being responsible for our part in the situation. God cannot come to our rescue when we have a victim mentality. Even when something seems out of our control and the bad thing that is happening to us is because of another's actions, there is always a lesson to learn. Keep your mind and attitude in a positive state so that God can help lift you up. "When you complain you remain, when you praise you are raised." (Joel Osteen)

Practice

Every morning invite God into your day. Ask him to show you his love and how you can further His Kingdom. Look at the challenging situations or trials that are happening in your life right now. Do you need to change your attitude about them so that God can work things out? What lesson are you to learn from them? Have you invited God into the situations/trials and turned it over to him to help you? Don't allow your failures to define you, allow them to refine you instead.

Stories of Confirmation:

Do It All Again

The trial I had to go through when I was 33 was the most difficult and challenging time of my life. However, if I could go back in time and change my choices to avoid going through my trial, I would not. I learned so much about myself and God because of it. My trial has refined me in so many ways and made me a better person. My spiritual crisis led me to a whole new understanding of God, and it prepared me to share my experiences through my teaching to benefit others. It has been a crucial awakening for my whole family. We all have stronger faith and are more spiritual. I have been able to share my lessons with my kids so they can learn from my mistakes. My trial also makes me know that whatever I am faced with, God will be walking right beside me, helping me through it all. What peace knowing that my Heavenly Father is in my corner. Together we can handle anything that comes my way!

It's Not How You Start That Matters

A friend of mine was born into rather, rough circumstances. His mom was only 14 when she gave birth to him and the father was nowhere to be found. His grandmother raised him along with his 8 aunts, 2 uncles and a little sister. When he was six years old, his mother uprooted him from his stable environment at his grandmothers and moved out on her own. So, began a rough road of watching his mom struggle to provide for them, and him struggling to find himself in a fatherless world where he had to grow up fast to be the man of the family. People made jest of him, both in school and at home because of his tall and lanky stature, and his pronounced stutter. He kept to himself and rarely spoke to avoid the constant teasing. His poor self-perception hindered his learning and he had to repeat the fifth grade. Everything was going wrong in his life until he found his saving grace through athletics. His stutter didn't matter on the court or in the field because he didn't have to talk. Even though athletics helped him get through junior high and high school a little easier, he still struggled to find himself.

His mother died of cancer when she was 33. He was only 19 and all alone trying to deal with his mom's death. He turned to drinking and womanizing to try to forget the pains of his life. A year later he met his wife and the mother of his 3 children. Together they had built the American dream, nice cars, a house in the suburbs, good jobs and a family. He thought his rough roads were all behind him. However, the final blow came when his wife asked for a divorce. He was devastated to think that his kids would have to live without a father in the home. The divorce was nasty and drove him to his breaking point. He felt like a failure.

It was at this exact time that he kept running into an old college classmate who had become a pastor. Somehow, he would see him many times a week. His friend would always invite him to church. It took him several months to accept his invitation; God knew he needed someone in his face nearly every day, so he arranged their meetings through serendipity. His divorce was too much for him to handle on his own. In his despair and state of hopelessness, he began to seek after God for help due to his pastor friend.

Looking back, my friend now understands that in all of his life's struggles, God was always trying to get his attention. He always tried to handle them on his own which in the end created more problems. It was when he turned to God for help that he finally received the love, support and guidance that he longed for his whole life. He also realized that God used his biggest failure to help refine and prepare him for the future. Today he is happy and successful. He uses his gifts to teach bible study groups in his home and his experiences to support others who are going through divorce. All of the hardships in life have value on the spiritual plane. God doesn't care where you start, he just wants you to finish with Him.

Two roads diverged in a wood, and I, I took the one less traveled by, and that has made all the difference.

– Robert Frost

LESSON 5

THE ROAD LESS TRAVELED

My journey thus far had awakened me to the fact that Twyla was just a messenger and that my real teacher is God. As I practiced Twyla's lessons and put those into action, God began to reveal himself to me a little at a time. He had built up my faith in all the ways he was partnering with me throughout my daily life. I became so excited about how He had transformed my life that I wanted to share the God that I knew with others. However, I soon began to realize that very few are willing to choose to go down the road less traveled. Fear of the unknown, giving up control, close mindedness, religious ideologies and ego are some of the road blocks that prevent people from knowing God in an intimate way.

Deciding to go down the road less traveled is choosing to seek a personal relationship with God. In today's world of instant gratification, entitlement, and lack of personal responsibility, it is no wonder that most take the easy road of the world. *"But small is the gate and narrow the road that leads to life and only a few find it."* (Mathew 7:14, NIV) What those who have taken the road less traveled know is, although it has twist, turns, trials and tribulations, it leads to a great supernatural life. Are you ready to choose the road less traveled and to invite God into your life? All you have to do is invite Him in with this simple prayer: **"Heavenly Father, I repent of my sins. Thank you for loving me and sending Your Son to die on the cross to cover all my sin, past,** *present and future. I accept you as my Lord and Savior and invite you to come into my life and make me new. I place my hope and faith in you, knowing you will guide me to fulfill the divine purpose you have for my life. I thank you, and I love you, in Jesus name, Amen.*" If you said that prayer, you are now beginning a supernatural journey, congratulations!

God has already started the journey by pursuing you and showing you that He is willing to be your teacher. All you have to do is; be a willing student. Begin by shifting your perspective to look at everything in your life in a spiritual way. Every circumstance and every person you have contact with are there to teach you something about yourself or are giving you an opportunity to respond to them in a spiritual way, with love. This is life school and the goal is to find the God within you. This may all seem a little difficult to think about, but you are not alone. God will equip you with the tools that you will need on the journey. When the student is ready, the right teacher appears. Teachers will come in the form of people, trials, books, songs, animals, angels, dreams, and other forms as well. Some teachers may be with you throughout your spiritual journey, while others may just pass through at the right time. You will recognize them when they arrive. When you open your mind up and seek from a spiritual perspective, the lessons and teachers flow in.

For me, Twyla showed up to mentor me. Even though we had been neighbors for two years prior to the beginning of my spiritual journey, she knew when I was ready. At just the right time, she began teaching me. She suggested that I should start reading spiritual books. She told me to go to the library or bookstore, and to ask Spirit to guide me to the book I was to read. Spirit answered, books fell off the shelves or caught my attention so that I knew it was the one for me. I read whatever book was sent- spiritual, religious, science, business, new age, psychology, history, and biographies all to quench my spiritual thirst. Sometimes a whole book would speak to me, while at other times, it might only be a chapter or a mere sentence that would resonate with my spirit.

No matter what teachers come along to help you in your spiritual journey, remember that just because something is outside the realm of your understanding today, it might not be in a few months or a year down the road. If you close your mind off to the possibilities, then you close off the learning process. Your spiritual journey then comes to a standstill. When I would come upon new information that I wasn't sure about, I would simply ask God for a confirmation. In a week or two as I contemplated it, God would always make it known to me.

Since every spiritual journey is unique, no two people experience the same lessons in the same way, it is important to understand that everyone is not at the same place spiritually. Some haven't started their journey, others maybe never will, some are farther down the path, while most are somewhere in between. Therefore, the spiritual understanding will not always be the same. All paths lead to God, but how one arrives there is up to individual choice. Understanding this alleviates much frustration and judgment. As I grew spiritually, I was no longer fulfilled in my church, so I looked for a church that was teaching more in-line with where I was on my spiritual journey. Be aware also, as you grow spiritually some friends will fall away while God will bring in new ones who are like- minded. As He expands you spiritually, He also expands your circle of influence as well, so that you can share what God is doing in your life. He also gives you discernment to know what you can share with others and what teachers are from God. Beware, some teachers teach falsely, or are out to make money off spiritual seekers. Hold every teacher and teaching up to God and he will make all things known to you.

The supernatural journey God has designed specifically for you does come with personal responsibility. He is your teacher now. In order for him to complete the divine design for your life you have to be a good student, be open to spiritual growth and correction. Growing spiritually is a lot like learning to read; in kindergarten, the teacher didn't teach the whole alphabet in a day. It was taught one letter at a time, the sounds, and visual representation. Once the letter was mastered, then the next letter was introduced. So it is with your spiritual learning. God only shows and teaches us what we are ready for. It is a journey where we are taking baby steps down the Path of Enlightenment. God introduces new ideas and shows Himself to us a little at a time. If He gave us loads of information too fast, we would become overwhelmed and close off the learning process, just as a kindergartener would do if the teacher taught the alphabet too fast. That being said, it is so important that with each lesson brought before us, we grasp it, let it become a stepping stone on our spiritual journey and implement it into our daily living.

Many times God will reveal to you the behaviors that are not serving your highest purpose. This is when He presents you with the opportunity for correction. Correcting your behavior helps with your spiritual growth. This is not usually an easy task. Most of the behaviors that need corrections are things we have been doing our whole life. Like a habit, it takes an effort to overcome and transform them.

Here is an example of one of the ways I needed correction. I was talking with a friend one day and she made a comment to me saying "Well I am not a pushover like you." She was not being mean spirited, but my feelings were hurt a little. However, I know God does not put me in circumstances and allow me to hear or see things without a purpose. He was revealing something to me. I began to contemplate her statement. Over the next week multiple situations arose where I became angry about how people in authority were not acting out of integrity toward the people they served. Where was this anger coming from? After much reflection and some discussion with one of my teachers, I understood that I had not stood up to the authority figures in my life when I disagreed with them and cowered down to their demands instead of being my true self. The correction; stop being a pushover! Now that I am aware of what is not serving my highest good, it is up to me as to whether I follow through and begin to stand up for myself.

Get out of God's Way

As you begin to travel down this spiritual road, you must remember the work God has done in you so far. As roadblocks appear, you will be tempted to justify away the miracles you have been shown and the seeds he has planted in you so far. In the following parable of the sower, Jesus describes the challenges facing those who come into this new knowledge of God.

"The farmer sows the word. Some people are like seed along the path, where the word is sown. As soon as they hear it, Satan comes and takes away the word that was sown in them. Others, like seed sown on rocky places, hear the word and at once receive it

with joy. But since they have no root, they last only a short time. When trouble or persecution comes because of the word, they quickly fall away. Still others, like seed sown among thorns, hear the word; but the worries of this life, the deceitfulness of wealth and the desires for other things come in and choke the word, making it unfruitful. Others, like seed sown on good soil, hear the word, accept it, and produce a crop some thirty, some sixty some a hundred times what was sown." (Mark 4:14-20, NIV)

You must be like the seed planted on fertile ground in order to experience God fully.

Practice

An exercise in using your spiritual perception: Think of a person or situation in your life that is causing you stress or discomfort. Look at them/ it with spiritual eyes to see what you are supposed to learn from them/ it. Do you need to correct your behavior? Is the behavior you are reflecting back to the person or situation of love? One of my teachers always reminds me, "What we resist persists". Many times, when we begin to understand the spiritual lesson we are to learn, then that which once caused stress and discomfort no longer exists.

Start drawing closer to God by adding a few spiritual practices into your daily/weekly routine and see how God is able to strengthen his connection with you. Here is a list of some things you can do to fertilize and care for your spirit while you are on your journey. Not everything listed is for everyone. Only try those things which interest or resonate with you. They are:

- ✓ Read spiritual books and texts
- ✓ start a yoga practice

- ✓ attend seminars/retreats
- ✓ meditate
- ✓ join a church
- ✓ do something creative
- ✓ pray
- ✓ volunteer
- ✓ martial arts/exercise
- ✓ balance body/mind/spirit
- ✓ dance
- ✓ watch spiritual television programs
- ✓ drumming circles
- ✓ healing modalities
- ✓ be still
- ✓ spend time with likeminded gatherings
- ✓ deep breathing
- ✓ spend time in nature
- ✓ study the Bible
- ✓ sing laugh/play

Stories of Confirmation:

Mirror Image for Change

  I know a lady that becomes red faced and angry when she hears someone gossiping. She will go on and on about how much she hates gossiping and about how terrible it is, you can see and hear the anger in her body and voice when she talks about it. The funny thing is - if she would look at her anger from a spiritual perspective, she would see that there is a lesson for her. When she is with her friends, guess what she does? She gossips. Not just a little, but a full out, on-slaughter of gossip, directed at whoever comes to mind, or whoever is in her line of vision. Spiritually, she is being shown that people gossiping are a mirror reflection of something she does not like about herself, so it makes her angry. If she would realize that there is a lesson for her, she would make a point to stop her habit of gossiping. If she understood that people gossiping are just reflecting her own actions, then she could learn her spiritual lesson and the anger would no longer come up. Most likely, gossip would no longer show up in her space. Anytime you are feeling strong, repetitive emotions, it's a pretty good sign that you might want to pause and look at things through spiritual eyes. Your spirit is trying to get your attention so that you can make a correction in yourself.

Horse Helper

  God sent me an unusual teacher during my refining period, a guy named Terry. Terry wasn't your typical guy. He was a horse, a black Tennessee walker. God brought him into my life quite unexpectedly and he was an outlet for high stress, and more importantly to help me find myself. I had ridden a horse only a couple of times, and Terry's owner was happy to teach me how to saddle and ride him. Right from the get-go, Terry challenged me - trying to do what he wanted, instead of what I wanted him to do. It was a lesson for me to take control instead of being controlled. On my first solo ride, he took off in a sprint, slammed on the brakes, and then spun me around trying to throw me off. He wanted to go back to the barn. I was scared to death, hung on for dear life, and yanked the reins to show him who was boss. From that day forward, I overcame my fear of horses and the fear of taking control. He and I became great buddies. Even though I didn't own him, anyone who saw me riding him would say "that is your horse." What they meant by that was, they could tell that Terry and I had a special bond beyond horse and rider. It was a spiritual connection. It was like he always knew what I needed when I came to the barn, and he always obliged. Without him, I probably would have gone off the deep end. I carried the lessons I learned from Terry over into my personal life to make it better. I stopped letting others control me, found myself, and took my power back. God sent me a teacher in the form of a horse!

You've got to Get Quiet

One of Twyla's favorite sayings is "you've got to get quiet". Twyla reminds me of this saying every time I visit her. What she means by this is that in order to hear God, you have to quiet your mind. Twyla is now 85 and has been bed ridden for ten years because of congestive heart failure. Twyla has always been a spiritual person, but being bed ridden has super-charged her connection with God. She spends many hours a day in spiritual practices of prayer, meditation, reading, and singing church hymns.

Being in "the quiet" is when she really hears God clearly. Although she is bed ridden, Twyla carries out a very special card ministry for God. Daily, she asks God who is in need of his touch and then the names just flow to her. She then writes a short note of encouragement to whomever God has placed in her heart. I have been on the receiving end of many of her cards and they always show up when I most need them. On top of that, what she writes always seems to hit home with what is happening in my life. Twyla is a great reminder of how when we get quiet and still, have a daily spiritual practice, we are able to hear Him more clearly. In turn we can be a blessing to others because we are able to hear his direction. My practice of being still for 30 minutes a day has been very beneficial in the writing of this book. I have received many topics, phrases, and chapter titles to guide me.

Wonder from Wendy's

In my family, all four of us kids worked at Wendy's while we were teenagers. My sister and I always talked about this nice couple who would come in on Sunday afternoons, decked out in their dancing costumes after a dance competition. Fast forward 15 years. My same sister pulls up to my house to pick up her kids after her hour commute from work. She has a book in her hand and gives it to me. There was a woman in the lobby doing a book signing when she had gotten off work, so she had picked up the book. After noticing it was a spiritual book, she figured she would give it to me since I was into "that stuff" and she was not. While we visited on my porch, she mentioned that the woman had looked so familiar, but neither of us recognized the author's name. However, as I flipped through the pages, there was a picture of the author in the back. I said to my sister, "This looks like the dancing lady from Wendy's." Neither of us had seen her since we were teens even though we lived in a small town, but both of us agreed that she was the one. I read her book and found it quite intriguing. A few weeks later I was at the store pushing my shopping cart around the corner and I rammed my cart into another. Who do you think was on the other end of that cart? Yep, it was the Wendy's lady and author. I apologized and then said, "By the way, I really enjoyed your book." I could tell she was taken aback by my comment. She went on to tell me that she uses a ghost name when she writes because she was afraid that the content of her book would cause her family troubles in the small town we dwelled. We talked a few more minutes and then she invited me to stop by her house sometime to converse some more. Gracie became another great teacher in my life all by Divine Design! Through her teachings, God really opened my eyes to how He is willing to work for me and through me. It has been such a blessing to know Gracie. To think that God was already lining up plans for my life when I was a 16-year-old worker at Wendy's blows me away! I am confident that He has done the same for you, keep seeking and He will begin unveiling His plans for you too.

All my life, my heart has yearned for a thing I cannot name.

– Andre Breton

LESSON 6

LOVE MAKES EVERYTHING SACRED

What is Love? Why does our heart and soul long for it? It is the greatest emotion, more easily experienced, than defined. How do you know when someone loves you? You know by their actions. They are there for you in good and in bad times, they show they genuinely care about you, they are affectionate with their words and actions, and they are honest, kind, respectful, and faithful. They allow you to be yourself, they will tough-love you when you need it, and they always want what is best for you. Love is an action word! God has already taken action to show us how much He loves us - by giving His Son up to death so that we can personally know Him. God's constant flow of love is supremely free and is His greatest gift. Through the hands-on learning. He has shown you that He is there for you and His actions are love.

Love is referenced in the Bible over 500 times, more than any other topic other than God, Jesus, and Heaven. Do you think there is a reason for that? Of course, it is no coincidence, because Love is God. His goal for us is to intimately know and share His love. All of God's laws and instruction can all be summed up with the word LOVE. Love makes everything sacred.

God's greatest commandment of all is as follows, "*Love the Lord your God with all your heart and with all your soul and with all your strength.*" (Deuteronomy 6:5, NIV) This is not a command to only love your Heavenly Father but to also love yourself. Scripture tells us that we are made in the image and likeness of the Father. "*On that day you will realize that I am in my Father, and you are in me, and I am in you*" (John14:20, NIV) Therefore, wouldn't it make sense that when you love yourself with all your heart and soul, that you are actually loving God? Today, begin to look at yourself from a spiritual perspective, love God with all your heart and soul, and love yourself with all your heart and soul. To do this, you must begin to look at yourself through the Eyes of Love and to make choices for your highest good. Sometimes the greatest gift of love you can give yourself is to protect yourself from those who try to influence you away from your greatest good. Negative peer pressure doesn't end after you make it through your teens. Many times, as adults, we have to distance ourselves from people who do not have the same values, those who put us down, or those who create constant drama. It is so important to surround yourself with people who are good to you. Look what the Bible says about the company we keep: "*Do not be misled: "Bad company corrupts good character.*" (1Corinthians 15:33, NIV) and also "*Do not make friends with a hot-tempered person, do not associate with one easily angered, or you may learn their ways and get yourself ensnared.*" (Proverbs 22:24-25, NIV) The company you keep matters greatly.

Obviously, as a human you are not perfect, and you are going to make mistakes and make choices that are not in your highest good. It is in those times, that you must step back, love yourself and God enough to learn from those mistakes, and then make corrections so you don't repeat them again. Once we are able to love ourselves, then we can fully love others. You can't give away something you don't have.

This brings us to another one of God's laws, "Love your neighbor as yourself." (James 2:8, NIV) This usually isn't too difficult if we like our neighbor, but where it becomes challenging is showing love to someone who has wronged us, to someone we don't actually like, or may not even know. If you begin to look at people through the spiritual Eyes of God, you begin to see that they are an image of God, just like you. It doesn't mean you have to hang around them or be their best friend. You don't have to love their actions; however, you can begin to love them anyway, showing them kindness instead of hatred. Again, look at the bigger picture to see the message behind their behavior. Are you to learn something from them? It is clear that God has a plan for everything, and all things work together for your greatest good, but sometimes we might not understand it at the time. Some of the most difficult people in my life have been there to facilitate change within me. There are no accidents or coincidences with God's work. He does everything with and for a Higher Purpose. When you choose to love yourself and others, you experience God's love more fully. *"I pray that out of his glorious riches he may strengthen you with power through his Spirit in your inner being, so that Christ may dwell in your hearts through faith. And I pray that you, being rooted and established in love, may have power, together with all the Lord's holy people, to grasp how wide and long and high and deep is the love of Christ, and to know this love that surpasses knowledge— that you may be filled to the measure of all the fullness of God."* (Ephesians 3:16-21, NIV)

Get out of God's Way

Most of us find it difficult to love ourselves. We have let negative thought patterns about ourselves, messages from our environment, and the media define us as something lesser than a spark off God's own flame. We are our own biggest critics; speaking words of hate, unworthiness, guilt, and shame over our lives. Deep down, we feel a void that we can't explain. Knowing that there is something more, but not understanding it is God's love that we are not accepting. Inevitably, what we do to fill the void of love for ourselves is to look outside of ourselves. However, no amount of money, popularity, beauty, toys, or love from others will ever be enough to fill the void.

It is so easy to get in the way of God's love by choosing actions that are not of love for ourselves or others. God has given us free will, to make our own choices. Every day, we make hundreds of choices, and make no mistake about it; every choice we make carries responsibility, even the little ones. Your choices have a ripple effect. Think about what happens when you drop a rock into a pond, the rock splashes in, and ripples go out from rock to change the water around it. So it is with our choices, every choice not only affects you, but also ripples out to affects others too. Your choices matter greatly. When we make choices for our highest good, we show ourselves love. The ripple effect sends out love to those around us also. When we choose to treat others with love, there is also a ripple effect of good that occurs from that action.

Unfortunately, most of us do not consider the power in our choices. We often make quick decisions or have reactive responses that carry a negative ripple effect. The following verses give instruction on transforming negative choices into right actions. "*Therefore, each of you must put off falsehood and speak truthfully to your neighbor, for we are all members of one body. In your anger do not sin': Do not let the sun go down while you are still angry, and do not give the devil a foothold. Anyone who has been stealing must steal no longer, but must work, doing something useful with their own hands, that they may have something to share with those in need. Do not let any unwholesome talk come out of your mouths, but only what is helpful for building others up according to their needs, that it may benefit those who listen. And do not grieve the Holy Spirit of God, with whom you were sealed for the day of redemption. Get rid of all bitterness, rage and anger, brawling and slander, along with every form of malice.*" (Ephesians 4:25-31, NIV) Negative choices such as these create holes in our aura of free will, where darkness fills in. The more holes and darkness we create, the harder it is for us to feel and see the light of God within us and within others. Through your negative choices, you actually move yourself toward darkness and away from Love.

Sometimes, we find ourselves at the mercy of the negative choices that others have made. Maybe you were raised by an alcoholic, drug user, child abuser, bully, or neglectful parent. Their choices have affected them and you greatly in all areas of life. Do not become a victim, turning your eyes upon yourself, and choosing to focus on the negative things you cannot control. Instead turn to God; He can help you heal those areas of your life that you have no control over. When we turn to Him during times of challenge, He is able to transform and cover us with His love. Rest assured, He will use the negative circumstances in your life to prepare you in some way to carry out the Divine Plan He has for you. Someone else's negative choices do not have to define your life!

Practice

Make a list of things you like about yourself and a list of things you do not like. Which list is longer? Take the "like" list and tape it to your mirror so that you can read it every day and add to it as you realize new things you like about yourself. Take the "do not like" list and scratch off those things you have no control over such as, eye color, height etc., look at the remaining items to see if you could turn them into small goals, and begin making changes with the things that are in your control. Focusing on the things that you like about yourself will increase your self-esteem. Ultimately, the goal is to love and accept yourself wholly and unconditionally just as God loves and accepts all of you, unconditionally.

Begin to be responsible for your choices and the ripple effect they have on your life and the lives of others. A simple shift in the intention of choosing to love in your actions will allow God to begin transforming your life and filling you up with His loving presence.

Look at the negative circumstances which are out of your control with a broader view. How could God be using those circumstances to prepare you for something greater? As an example, think of someone who was abused as a child by a family member. In the natural, it is a heart-breaking situation to put a child through. However, looking at the bigger picture, it is well known that abuse puts multiple generations in bondage by the repeated patterns passed down time and again. What if the child's purpose, born into an abusive family, was to break the bondage of abuse for future generations? One child's experience with abuse, and refusing to pass it on, saves all future generations in his family line by breaking the cycle of abuse. From a spiritual perspective, the child had a big purpose and carried it out.

Stories of Confirmation

Trying to Fill in the Void

Todd, a childhood friend, was in town and was looking forward to a night out with my sister and some of their mutual friends. Todd is one of those guys who has been blessed in his life. Physically, he is healthy, tall, and good looking. In his profession, he is respected and very successful. In his personal life, he has a beautiful and sweet girlfriend of many years. Todd and his girlfriend have really nice cars, a beautiful home, enough money to buy lots of toys, and travel often; Todd pretty much has a life that most would think is great. He is a small-town boy that has done well, and he is comfortable with his success. Todd thoughtfully, shows up to pick my sister and their friends up in a limo, because he doesn't want anyone drinking and driving. The night gets going and soon Todd becomes the life of the party, throwing back way too many beverages. As he drinks, he begins to name drop a little, and brag about his travels. By the end of the night, Todd is pretty smashed and as he climbs into the limo with my sister. His true feelings begin to come out. He starts saying to his girlfriend, "Tell me I am good enough, tell me they all like me, and tell me you love me." Over and over he repeated himself, as if a child seeking the approval of a parent. My sister's heart broke for Todd, knowing that he has been trying to fill the void in his life with worldly possessions, obviously, to no avail. It was difficult for my sister to witness the brokenness of a successful man. Todd is a great example that no matter how much success or stuff we acquire, it never makes us feel complete. Only God's love can do that.

Self-hate to Self-love

  Laura walked in the first day of class and quietly took a seat in the back of the room. She was dressed in all black, with heavy black eye makeup, and no smile upon her face. I always notice kids who need attention and soon was engaging her in small talk before class. I found out over the course of the next few weeks, that she was new to town and lived in the children's home that served teens that were removed from their homes because of abuse. She was a very bright student and had a gift for writing. As the semester progressed, she became more vocal in class and began to come out of her shell. One day, the lesson was on the importance of self-esteem and loving yourself; something many teens struggle with. I feel it is important to equip my students with techniques to help strengthen their self-esteem. Laura raised her hand and shared with the class that she comes from a rough upbringing. She went on to say that she hated herself because of things that had happened in her home, and she mentioned, that she abused herself through drug use, self-mutilation, sexual promiscuity, and even tried to take her life. Laura told the class that thanks to a technique a counselor shared with her, she was actually able to begin to love herself and stop the self-abuse. The counselor told her to write down three things she liked about herself, but Laura could only think of one; "I have pretty eyes." She then placed this on the mirror where she got ready in the morning and read it every day. Eventually, she was able to think of something else she liked and added it to her list. Before long, she was adding another and another. She told the class that if that technique could help her love herself, it could help anyone. Laura moved the following year, but I am certain that today she is a successful young lady. She stepped up to help herself, instead of becoming a victim, and letting her family's poor choices define her life. She also became a teacher and a role model to her peers that day.

Mr. Do Right

When my kids were little, I tried to help them learn right from wrong with a character I made up called Mr. Do Right. I taught them that Mr. Do Right lived in their head and he always was there to tell them the right thing to do if they would stop and ask. I would often ask them this question, "What would Mr. Do Right say?" Today, when I think of Mr. Do Right, I believe it is applicable to all of us. Mr. Do Right is your spirit. Your spirit is connected to God, who is love. Therefore, we all intrinsically know what choice the best is, to show love for ourselves or for others. When we choose love, we choose the light of God, and we attract more of the same into our lives. Listen to your own Mr. Do Right.

Choices Matter

Jimmy was that freshman who looked like a Greek God. He was handsome, a varsity athlete, a straight A student, and had an amazing personality. He came from a nice family and really had a lot going for him. Because of his maturity, the senior girls took notice of him, and before long he was hanging out with mostly upper classman. As a freshman, he wasn't really ready for the pressure that came with hanging out with seniors. Before long, he was going to all the parties and partaking heavily in the party scene. By sophomore year he stopped playing sports and his main activity was partying. He was so bright that he was still able to keep up his grades, so it seemed that there were no harmful consequences of his partying choices. By junior year, he was smoking pot pretty heavily. His appearance began to deteriorate, and he began to further neglect his schoolwork. When senior year rolled around, his peers were making plans for their future, but Jimmy was still choosing the party scene and had moved on to cocaine and other drugs. After Jimmy barely graduated high school, he went to work at McDonalds. He continued to hang out with the party crowd and met a party girl whom he eventually married and continued to do drugs with. When they had their first child, the baby was born with birth defects that required many surgeries and extra care. Jimmy tried to be a good husband and father, but could not break his drug addiction, so eventually he and his wife divorced. Jimmy struggled to hold down a job, and his once intelligent brain was burnt from his drug use, leaving him with few work options. Today, Jimmy is living a life that he was not destined for. He had so much potential, but instead of living into his full potential, he is living a life designed by poor choices. Spirit tried to get his attention many times and still does through some pretty tough consequences, but Jimmy continues to ignore Spirit's call. Unfortunately, many others have been affected by the ripple effect of his choices too. God still loves Jimmy, but because of his destructive actions and lifestyle, he has created a life of continual struggle and separation between himself and God. It saddens me to think about what the ripple effect of Jimmy's life could have been, compared to what it has been. A simple shift of his choices would have allowed him to live into his full potential as one of God's children. In order to realize our God given destiny, we have to follow spirit's lead when making choices. God can't get us there by Himself; we have to co-create our lives by making good choices. Every choice matters!

"Only spiritual consciousness – realization of God's presence in oneself and in every other living being – can save the world. I see no chance for peace without it. Begin with yourself. There is no time to waste. It is your duty to do your part to bring God's kingdom on Earth."

– Paramahansa Yogananda,

LESSON 7

HOLDING THE SPACE

When you fully begin to seek the ways of God, more will be asked of you and more will be revealed to you. That is, if you hold the space to allow spirit to flow into and out of you. Holding the space is living out God's spiritual laws in your daily life. You must walk the walk. Thankfully, He only has a few laws which cover everything on the earthly plane. First, you must love God with all your heart, your entire mind and all your soul. He is the first before: your family, your job, money or any material possessions. Second, you must love your neighbor as yourself. That means everyone you meet, the difficult family member, the annoying co-worker, and the homeless beggar on the street. Loving everyone as God sees them, without judgment. Lastly, you reap what you sow. Again, you have free will choice and consequences that are determined by those choices. Living by God's spiritual laws brightens you, and because you are holding a space of love for others. People around you are going to have to brighten also or move away. Energetically, people will be able to feel a difference in you as you live out God's laws.

One word of caution about holding a loving space it does not mean that you become a push over, let people walk on you, or stop the expression of your emotions. You can love all people and still disagree with their actions. It is important that you allow yourself full expression. You can fully express yourself in a loving way. Of course, people will still get mad at you and try to manipulate you by accusing you of not being "Godly" when you disagree with them. Stand your ground confidently, lovingly and bless them.

As you live in alignment with God, your connection to him becomes clearer. You are able to "hear" him better. The hearing may be in an audible voice, an intuition, through a dream or other ways. Be open to his promptings and follow through on what is asked of you. God wants you to help him further his kingdom here on earth if you so choose. Living this way takes faith. Especially when things seem impossible in the natural or when you do not understand why God is asking you to do something. One time as I was paying for my iced tea at a drive-up window, I was prompted to buy the person's order that was behind me. I don't know why I was asked to do that, but I did it anyway. Maybe that person was having a bad day or maybe he or she needed to feel loved. We are not always going to understand God's ways but when you are willing to walk with him, you will have the faith that nothing happens without his greater purpose in mind. As you take care of God's children, he in turn blesses you in magical ways and life becomes unbelievably miraculous, so fun and full of joy.

Get out of God's Way

We have already established that nothing can separate us from God's love and his pursuit of us. However, living out God's laws on a daily basis is very challenging. No one is perfect. During these times of imperfection, we may feel in limbo because we are unable to hear God clearly. You may even find yourself asking "God, can you hear me now?" Our connection is weakened because of sin. Sin is missing the mark. Luckily for us, Jesus covers our sin past, present and future. God forgives us and loves us regardless of our sin. God doesn't punish us for our sins but does allow us to reap the consequences of it. However, sin creates separation from God. In order to get the clear connection back, we have to realign ourselves with God. How is this done? Since we all miss the mark at times, the trick is to acknowledge and take responsibility for it. Sometimes we feel sorry for our sin because we have gotten caught or because the consequences are too tough. True repentance biblically means to "change one's mind". To truly be sorry for our sin means that we are genuinely disappointed in our actions and are willing to make changes in our thinking which translates to changes in our behavior.

Often times our sin is a result of ingrained habits and thought patterns that we have been doing our whole lives. We cannot overcome our sin on our own. We need God's grace. Prayer is a great tool to assist us in receiving his grace and conquering our habitual sin. When you notice an area where sin is prevalent in your life, prayer is needed to assist you in breaking the habit. Prayer can break the chains of sin, even a prayer as simple as *"Thank you Father for bringing my sin to my attention. Please help me to transform my old patterns of thinking to align with your laws of love. In Jesus name I pray, Amen"*.

Willful and perpetual sin has severe consequences. It fills our spirit with darkness. Perpetual darkness draws in evil influences. What are evil influences? Evil influences can come in multiple forms. They may be people who try to influence us in negative ways or through negative thought patterns that get in the way of fulfilling your destiny. They might be ghosts that try to keep us in a state of fear or they might be dark or evil spirits, demons, or fallen angels called unholy angels. Evil influences might show up as the darkest of dark, the Biblical Satan, or the Devil. No matter which form of evil appears in our lives, the Bible is very clear on the danger of their influences and tells us to be on guard. *"Be sober-minded; be watchful, your adversary the devil prowls around like a roaring lion, seeking someone to devour."* (1Peter 5:8, NIV) "Put on the full armor of God, so that you can take your stand against the devil's schemes." (Ephesians 6:11, NIV) Every day there is a battle between good and evil, both are trying to occupy your soul. The danger comes when we perpetually choose evil. This removes us from God's protection and our soul fills up with darkness.

When we sin through our thoughts, words, or actions we open ourselves up for attack from dark and evil influences. Attack comes in the form of physical, mental, spiritual and social problems. When you begin to notice a problem in any of these areas, you can appeal to God for protection by saying the following deliverance prayer: *"Father, if there are any unholy ones in, on, near, or around me I nail, hold them fast, and silence them. I decommission, bind, and encapsulate them all through the Power of the Shed Blood of The Lamb and I bring them up immediately to you Father to deal with as you see fit. I call in all holy angels and guides to battle, protect, and defend against the unholy ones, so that all who come against must either be transformed or moved away. May you fill any empty place or lonely space within me and around me with your Love and your Light in Jesus name I pray, Amen."*

I often start my day off with this prayer to set the protective boundary around myself. The good news is that if we walk in the light, darkness has no authority. When we choose love, the Light of God protects us from the evil forces.

Our egos can also hinder our connection to God. The ego is always looking out for "number one" and this way of living is reinforced in our entitlement society. As a teacher, I would pose this simple question to my students. What is stealing? They would respond, "Taking something that doesn't belong to you." They all agreed that stealing was wrong. Then I would make the following statement, "You go to lunch at McDonalds and pay with a ten-dollar bill. The lady at the cash register gives you change for a twenty. What do you do?" To my surprise, over 80% of all my high school students over a seven-year period said they would keep the money. When I asked them why they would keep it, most would say things like, "it's her fault" or "my lucky day." The thing I found even more surprising was that most didn't think that keeping the money was stealing! I reminded them about their own definition of stealing and still they justified their actions. That is entitlement, thinking you deserve something for nothing. When we begin to feel entitled, we take our eye off of God and put it on ourselves. It is hard to follow God if you take your eyes off of Him. When we put our eyes on ourselves, ego steps in to run our life and Edges God Out. Recognize when you begin to have an entitlement mentality and put your eyes back on God. It might be easier to follow ego, but when you choose to follow God the rewards are so much greater.

Practice

How are you being? Begin to take notice of how you are being in all situations and toward all people in your daily living. Observe yourself, your thoughts, actions, motives and emotions as you move through the day. Are you being love? When you recognize you have missed the mark, make correction, so as not to allow darkness and evil to permanently reside in your soul. Keep your eye on God and ego in its place.

Stories of Confirmation

Texas or Bust

When my daughter Lainey was a junior in college, she started talking about moving to Texas when she graduated. Lainey had visited Texas once for a 3-day weekend with friends and immediately felt drawn to it. When anyone would ask her "why Texas" she would always say "I just know I am to go there, they (Texans) are my people." Shortly before graduation, she and I took a trip to Texas to get a feel for where she would like to live, Austin or San Antonio. We visited each city and she really didn't feel drawn to either. We decided to check out all the towns in between. We drove from town to town exploring each one. After the first ten minutes in New Braunfels, TX she said, "this is it, this is where I am going to live."

Everyone was surprised that a young girl would move 13 hours from home to a strange town, without a job, or a place to live, or even one person she knew. However, Lainey had faith that God would work everything out for her since she was willing to follow the guidance, he was giving her through intuition and signs of confirmation. In June after graduation, Lainey and one of her girlfriends, Allie went back to Texas. Allie had worked as a sales rep in Texas a few years prior to their visit. She was excited to show Lainey her favorite dance halls and introduce her to some of the people she had met there. Lainey returned home elated, God had begun finishing what he had started in her life. That week she was hired on the spot at a nursing job fair, a family offered to let her stay in their home for six weeks, for free, if she would house sit for them while they were out of town, she made many friends and had two guys who wanted to take her on a date when she moved to Texas. Any doubts Lainey might have had about moving to Texas were put to rest as God effortlessly made all the arrangements that were necessary to get her there. I know God had Lainey move to Texas for a reason even though that still remains to be seen. Lainey did a great job of not getting in God's way by worrying about all the necessities of life she would need while in Texas. She had complete faith that He would work everything out. So, He did.

Testing Her Faith

God had really been teaching my friend Ava and she was really growing spiritually. She felt close to God for the first time in her life and really started to understand the importance of having faith in Him. Just as she was coming into these realizations, she found that things were not going so well in her life. As she was sitting in her apartment one night, she heard God tell her to tithe the last $25 she had to her name. Of course, she immediately thought that it was a crazy idea because she had no food and no toilet paper. However, she chose to have faith and gave away the last of her money. She went to bed that night hungry and not knowing where she was going to get the funds she needed to live on. The next day she received an unexpected $1300 check in the mail. God knew the check was on the way, but he was testing her faith to see if she would follow through on what was asked of her even though from a human perspective it seemed like a horrible idea. Ava was relieved to get the check and thanked God for His unending supply. This test of faith was a major turning point in Ava's life and in her walk with God. Ava no longer worried about money and had complete faith in God's direction for her life. God continues to bless her above her wildest expectations because she lives by God's laws of love and has strong faith in Him.

It is easy to have faith in what God is doing in your life when everything is going well. When things get tough, God is watching to see if we will continue to trust and rely on him. Doing so, shows God that your relationship with Him is top priority and allows for further intimacy with Him.

Fear No Evil

My son Kenny was home from college and came barging into my room one night around 3 o'clock in the morning. He jumped in between my husband and me, like a little kid and was shaking uncontrollably. He told me that just as he was almost asleep demons began screaming in his ear. He said he couldn't move and that the demons were trying to terrorize him. It was the scariest thing that had ever happened to him. I knew the devil had visited him because of how he was trembling as a 21-year-old. Also, at the time, Kenny was just beginning to understand that he has a calling on his life and will be stepping into some sort of leadership role to further God's kingdom. I am certain the devil was trying to scare him into staying "asleep" and not waking up to the calling on his life. As he trembled beside me, he was afraid to go to sleep because he thought the demons might return. We said the prayer of protection and he soon fell fast asleep.

Empty Nest, Almost

Our baby girl was in her last semester of high school and would be heading off to college the following fall. For me and my husband, it was kind of bitter sweet. Although we love our kids and miss them when they are gone, we were actually looking forward to the empty nest. We started having children young and were excited to finally have "our time" after 24 years of raising kids. Personally, this would be the first time that I could pursue my own interest without having the daily responsibilities of motherhood. In my mind I would be spending my days writing, reinventing myself and drawing closer to God through study and spending quiet time with him. God had other plans!

The previous summer God had brought a new friend from California, Julia into my life through unusual circumstances. When we first met, we both knew that our connection was divine but were unsure what plans God had for our friendship. Over the course of the next six months we kept in touch and strengthened our connection. In January I received a distraught phone call from Julia. She was sobbing into the phone explaining that the guy she lived with and had planned to marry after the birth of their child had decided he wasn't ready to be a husband or a father. She had just packed all her stuff into her car and was driving because she had nowhere to go, little money and an ex who had no care for her or their baby's wellbeing. As we discussed her options, I realized that the only one she had was to move in with her grandma and sleep on her couch. Her pregnancy was making her so sick that she couldn't even work to support herself. After talking to my husband about her situation, we decided to offer to have her move in with us. We were all hesitant at first. She would have to drive across the country and move from the bustling LA life style to a small Midwestern town of 13,000 leaving behind friends, her grandma and warm weather for snow and freezing temperatures. We were almost empty nesters and would be taking on her, a future baby, and a financial increase. We all chose to have faith in what God had started and placed our trust in him.

We all had quite an adjustment the first month and still were not sure how God would provide but knew he would. The following month Julia and I each received a letter in the mail with a $14,000 check! An acquaintance of mine knew that Julia needed financial assistance for herself and her baby and also sent me money to help cover the cost of our added expenses. Needless to say, we were both blown away by her generosity and by God's provision. When we called to thank her, she said "don't thank me, thank Father, it was His idea."

Julia has lived with us for 7 months and has become part of our family. We have been able to provide her with a place to stay and family support and in turn she has been such a blessing to our whole family. It has been a testimony to all of us that when you follow God's lead, he will make a way even when it looks impossible from the human perspective.

"Once you feel what it means to live in a state of bliss, you will love it. You will know that Heaven on Earth is truth—that Heaven truly exists. This way of life is possible and it's in your hands. Moses called it the Promised Land, Buddha called it Nirvana, Jesus called it Heaven, and the Toltecs call it a New Dream."

– Don Miguel Ruiz

PART II

CO-CREATION

Co-Creation

The second half of this book will teach you how to partner with God in the process of co-creating your life. The co-creation process is an everyday choice you make to design the life you desire with God's help. God loves us so much and wants us to have our hearts desires. Some may think that co-creating is materialistic and selfish. As with all things, co-creation can be misused if you place more importance on your desires than God's will for your life. Those who are consistently seeking him for the right reasons will find their heart's desires align with God's desires for their lives. Co-creation is another stepping stone to knowing God more fully. He is willing to co-create with anyone who is willing to partner with him in the process.

The co-creation process uses proven techniques such as positive thinking, prayer, visualization and manifestation. When there is a partnership with God, these techniques are amplified and have no limits. Co-creation begins with the realization that you are responsible for your life and that you have the power of God at your disposal because He is within you. Your soul or inner voice then begins to prompt you to follow the desires of your heart and your passions. This new inspiration calls you to action to produce a mutually valued outcome for you and God. It is the actions of your mind, eyes, and mouth that facilitate the co-creation process. Each works independently but each influences the other greatly. In order for God to do all he wants to do in your life, you must have a clear understanding of how your mind, eyes and mouth work in the co-creative process.

"The game of life is a game of boomerangs. Our thoughts, deeds and words return to us with astounding accuracy."

– Florence Shovel Shinn

LESSON 8

YOUR MIND

The co-creation process begins in the mind with your thoughts. Our thoughts are like a key that unlocks all possibility. I liked to demonstrate the power of thought to my classes by giving them a weighted chain. I would have them hold the chain between their thumb and forefinger with their elbow resting on their desk, and then I would tell them to focus their thought to make the weight sway forward and backwards. As the weight would begin to follow their thought, I would then have them switch their thought to have it swing from side-to-side or in a circle. As the weight swung, I would have them interject the repeating thought of, "Stop, stop, stop," and the weight would come to a standstill. Next, I would have them swing the weight in any direction prompted by their thought. When the weight was in motion, they interjected the thought over and over, "I can't swing the weight, and my weight won't swing." The weight would come to a complete stand still. Being teenagers, they were always so blown away because they did not understand the mind-body connection. Through this activity, the kids were able to see how the body is affected by thought and especially how a negative thought has the capability to block normal body functions. Try this for yourself with a necklace or a string tied to something weighted, and you too will see the power of your thoughts in action.

Science has proven that our thoughts affect our physical bodies. Quantum physics proves that everything in the universe is energy in motion. Your thoughts also carry energy and are capable of influencing all of God's creations. God created the laws of nature that science has proven, and they are meant to be utilized. The term associated with one of God's Universal Laws is the law of attraction. It is important to keep an open mind, especially my Christian readers. I realize that many different groups and teachers have taught the law of attraction. However, not many teach that the law of attraction works because of the partnership with God. The law of attraction begins with your thoughts and involves tapping into the Divine Mind of God.

We apparently have between 50,000-70,000 thoughts a day according to Bruce Davis, Ph.D. (Huffington Post 7/23/2013) That is crazy to comprehend but every thought matters to your life. You do not have to keep track of all the thousands of thoughts, but it is important to begin to notice what the majority of them are focusing on. Ideally, our thoughts should be focused on love rather than fear, the positive rather than the negative, on opportunities rather than limitations, and the specifics of what kind of life you want to co-create with God. These kinds of thoughts carry a high energy frequency and attract similar energies to you. If you are focusing on opportunities, love, and on the positive, you will attract more opportunities, more love and more positive things into your life. However, throughout the day, many of our thoughts are negatives; fear, hate, jealously, shame, limitations etc.... These are all considered negative thought patterns and will attract like energies, fearful situations, hateful and jealous people and limited opportunities. Thankfully, negative thoughts carry low frequencies and therefore are slower to manifest in our lives. Positive thoughts have higher energy frequencies and manifestation is much quicker.

Take a minute to think about what is going on in your life right now. What kind of energy are you attracting to your life from your thoughts? Another way to help you notice where the majority of your thoughts are is to look at the circle of friends you have. If most are negative in their actions and attitudes, then the majority of your thoughts are sending out a negative frequency. Therefore, you attract negative people to yourself. The opposite is true if your friend group is positive in actions and attitudes. You will attract positive people and circumstances to yourself. There are some of you that may be thinking, well my friend so and so is negative, and I am not. Sometimes we will have a friend or two that are opposite to us, energetically speaking. However, if you can spend long periods of time with them without feeling worn out, that is your clue that you are not being honest with yourself; you are just like them. Opposite energies are going to repel each other, so spending too much time with someone who is an opposite energy is going to physically and mentally weigh you down.

Most people find that they give more attention to negative thoughts than to positive ones. That is because we are imperfect humans. Once people begin to understand how the law of attraction works, they begin to take steps to move away from focusing too much on the negatives around them. They then will begin to use the law of attraction to their advantage. You can do the same. Doing so is going to take intention and practice to develop the mental muscle needed for positive co-creation. Your mind is an instrument of God, and it is your choice as to whether you use it to bless or curse your life.

The Divine Mind

The Divine Mind is the mind of God that resides deep within us. Some have termed it the superconscious. It is that space where the thoughts are all loving. Turn your thoughts to yourself to get a comparative analogy of the concept of the Divine Mind. Some thoughts that come to mind for me are along these lines. "My butt is getting soft," "I should be doing more", "I have probably screwed up my kids in some way," "I hate those darn wrinkles" All these thoughts come from the conscious mind or carnal mind, the mind of the world. The carnal mind tends to hold the standards that society tells us about what we should be like and takes advantage of our insecurities. These thoughts when repeated over and over move into the subconscious where they begin to manifest in our life. Subconscious thought patterns are very powerful but usually lack positive direction. When we allow the subconscious to work without direction, we end up manifesting the thought patterns that we have allowed to be embedded there. Thoughts from others and yourself such as: "I'm stupid" "I'm never going to amount to anything", "I'm ugly" "No one will ever want me" "I'm just like my mother/father." Over time we begin to believe and subconsciously live out those thoughts. Unfortunately, most of our conscious and subconscious thoughts about ourselves tend to be more negative than positive. Thoughts from the Divine Mind are like this; "I am beautiful just as I am" "I am enough", "I am perfectly and wonderfully made" "I love you unconditionally". There is no judgment or work you have to do in the presence of the Divine Mind. The Divine Mind wants the best for you and is available to help co-create the life of your dreams. Read on to find out how.

Guard Your Mind

The first step to co-create with the Divine Mind is to begin to guard your mind from negative influences. This is a choice you make in your conscious mind about what thoughts you are going to let fill your head. The propensity of the conscious mind is to be influenced by the ways of society, and the Bible refers to this as being carnal minded. *"Do not conform to the pattern of this world but be transformed by the renewing of your mind. Then you will be able to test and approve what God's will is-his good, pleasing and perfect will."* (Romans 12:2, NIV) This verse reminds us to not be influenced by the world in our thoughts but to rather strive to connect with the Divine Mind and be transformed. One aspect of guarding your mind is to basically find a positive perspective in any negative thought pattern you are having. It is a choice to shift focus from that which is causing suffering to a positive overriding thought. Sometimes it might require turning negativity over to God and having faith that he will work everything out to your favor in his time. In order to guard your mind, you have to begin to recognize when your thoughts are negative and change the negative thought pattern to positive one. For example, my youngest daughter was recently treated very unfairly by an adult. His actions have caused her much heartache and disappointment. As her mother when I think of this situation my carnal mind goes to a place of anger and dislike toward this adult. To guard my mind, I have to focus on a thought that is in line with the Divine Mind such as "I do not understand why this is happening but I will put my trust in God to work this situation out in my daughters favor" or "I have faith that there is a bigger plan at work here." It is not always easy; sometimes you have to battle with your carnal mind all day long. However, if we give in to the carnal mind, then we begin to attract negative situations into our lives. Doing so blocks the Divine Mind from working for our greatest good.

Another aspect of guarding your mind is to recognize what you are allowing to influence your thoughts. What you see and hear in your environment can have both positive and negative influences on your thoughts. It is important to become mindful of what you are allowing into your conscious mind. Viewing, reading and listening to a lot of garbage on TV, radio, internet and in magazines can de-sensitize us, and can negatively influence our thoughts and values. This can be a slippery slope because most media today has a lot of sexual and violent content. You don't have to avoid all media, but you have to recognize if what you are watching and listening to is influencing you negatively. I for one had to stop watching Desperate Housewives and stop reading Cosmopolitan magazine. I noticed I was entertaining thoughts and justifying potential actions that went against my values. The perpetual viewing and listening to darkness, brings darkness into our thoughts which brings darkness into our actions. Your darkness repels and moves the light of God away. Guard your mind from the darkness in the media and society which has become so prevalent.

Lastly, to prepare the mind for co-creation with the Divine Mind, some house cleaning must take place. Everyone has negative thought patterns buried deep within their subconscious which have taken root throughout their life because of childhood experiences. We may have taken on wrong belief systems from our parents or heard repeated negative comments about ourselves that we believe are true. These negative thought patterns hinder you and must be acknowledged and cleansed in order to come into alignment with Divine Mind. Doing so allows you to realize all of God's power and love.

Your emotions are the signals that let you know what house cleaning needs to be done on the subconscious level. We all feel negative emotions at times but begin to notice repetitive negative emotions that show up time and again. Repetitive negative emotions are signals from your spirit that some inner work needs to be done. The most common negative emotions are shame, sadness, guilt, anger, fear, anxiety and jealously. First, you want to identify the emotion and allow yourself to feel it. Allowing yourself to feel a negative emotion can be painful. Some people make the mistake of covering up the emotion through medications or by pushing the emotion back down, so they don't have to face the pain. This is when guarding your mind actually acts as a way to suppress the signal. If you keep the emotion suppressed, it is still going to come up and eventually will come out sideways through negative actions, physical or emotional illness or a dark night of the soul. So, you have a choice, to either live with the negative emotion knowing it is causing you harm in your mind, body, and spirit or face it head on. Facing your strong emotions is scary because suppressed memories might have to be worked through. You have to be vulnerable, letting go of the need to control the emotion. Some people are able to do this through inner reflection and relying on God for a healing, but those who have had very strong negative emotional events in their lives might need assistance. I highly recommend seeking out a spiritual counselor or mentor to give you a spiritual perspective on what you are going through. Cleansing the subconscious is usually not an enjoyable experience. However, when we take the time to clean those negative emotional triggers out of our subconscious mind, it is life transforming. It also serves as a springboard to new spiritual awareness and intimacy with God.

Get out of God's Way

Since co-creation begins with a partnership of your mind and the Divine Mind, you can get in the way by choosing to not consider the condition of your mind. Disregarding the importance of your thoughts and the energy they carry is irresponsible. By choosing not to take command of your thoughts, a life lived on "auto pilot" is created. On auto pilot it is easy to become a victim and to be reactive of life instead of being an active cocreator. Some people live their life this way because they feel they are not worthy to live the life of their dreams. The unworthiness can stem from their past actions or because of the wrong messages they accepted as truths from their environments while growing up. Let me remind you that you are worthy because you are a child of the Most High! Even in Jesus's family line, there were reasons that he could have felt unworthy. His family line contained a prostitute named Rahab and a murderer named King David. If God can bring the savior of the world, Jesus, out of that genealogical line, then there is nothing He can't do for you also. Living your life on auto pilot does not allow God to show you the full measure of His love. Your heavenly Father wants to co-create the life of your dreams!

Choosing to ignore or medicate the strong negative emotions creates a ticking time bomb within. The time bomb is reflected in external turmoil. "**As within, so without; any in harmony on the external indicates there is mental in**

harmony" (Florence Shovel Shinn). You must be willing to face "the demons" within so that your mind can align with the Divine Mind for transformative co-creation.

Practice

Face any reoccurring negative emotion, by spending time reflecting on why it keeps reappearing and taking steps to heal the experience that created it. Seek professional help if needed. This will remove any road blocks in the co-creative process. Start today to reflect on what kind of thoughts you are giving the most attention to. Practice guarding your mind when you recognize a thought that is not in line with your highest good. Begin the co-creative process by being responsible with your thoughts, focusing on the things you want to manifest in your life.

Stories of Confirmation:

From Hater to Friend

Heather's co-worker, Pete, always seemed to find a problem with how Heather did her job. Pete was critical of Heather to her peers, and always gave her correction about what he thought she should be doing daily. After a while Heather's co-workers were asking her why Pete was always picking on her. Heather had no idea and had really never had much interaction with him. After a few weeks Heather began to think about what Pete was going to say or do to her every day. When she came home from work her husband would even ask what Pete did to her that day. Needless to say, the more she focused on Pete's negative behavior toward her the more negative behavior she received. Finally, after weeks of dreading going to work because of Pete, Heather decided to change her thoughts of him. She began to focus on his good quality (she could only think of one) instead of thinking about the negative comments that he usually gave her. The first couple of days, Heather really had to guard her mind when she saw him and especially when he made one of his condescending comments toward her about how she was doing her job. Heather pressed on with her positive thoughts and after the first week of guarding her mind, it seemed as if Pete was actually being nicer toward her. Before long Heather found that Pete was a really nice guy but was very insecure at his job because he was not very bright. Pete was trying to offset his own insecurities by pointing out problems with Heather to make himself feel better. A simple shift in Heather's thoughts about Pete sent off a loving high energy which is what she received back from him. Today Heather and Pete work alongside each other on many projects and get along great. This story is a great reminder of what you think about you bring about.

Emotional Turmoil

A young man named Sal has been a gifted athlete since grade school. It was common for him to train with the high school teams when he was in junior high. At that young age he was already equal to or better than most of the high school boys. His parents were divorced, and he and his Dad bonded through athletics. When he got to high school as a freshman, he surrounded himself with kids who were athletes and who were making good choices in their activities outside of school. He participated in sports and had a pretty successful year as a freshman athlete. By his sophomore year, he was teetering between his athletic friend group and a new group of kids who were smoking pot. Sal began to miss practices here and there and didn't seem to be taking his athletics as serious as before. In that same year, his mother suddenly died.

When Sal returned to school after the funeral, he began gravitating toward the pot smoking crowd. His grades started dropping and he quit playing sports. Many coaches and teachers tried to intervene on his behalf and talked to him about the poor decisions he was making. Everyone knew he was hurting from his Mom's death, and he was self-medicating through pot smoking to deal with his hurt. Sal confided to his coach that his Mom had committed suicide, and that his Dad had little to do with him because he spent all his time with a new girlfriend. Everyone tried to get him to see a counselor to help him deal with his loss, but he refused. When confronted about his pot smoking, he claimed to have everything under control, yet he was nearly failing all his classes and smoking every day.

By the time junior year rolled around, he had started taking other drugs. Sal had a scare and was rushed to the ER and then entered rehab. Once out of rehab, teachers once again came to his aid to try to help him by offering to get him back into sports and reminding him that he would have to switch his friend group if he was going to be successful staying clean. Sal kept the same friends and before long was back to smoking pot but swearing off other drugs for the rest of his life. Fast forward 3 months, and he was rushed back to the ER and stayed in the hospital for a week. The doctors were not sure if his brain was going to recover from the drug use and worried about him becoming brain dead. Luckily, he came out of it and went back to rehab. He returned to school again but ended up dropping out. He continued to hang out with the same friends and the self-destructive pattern continued.

Sal is a great example of someone who is running from their pain instead of facing it. Because he keeps running and self-medicating, he keeps making choices that are not for his highest good and keeps attracting negative situations and people into his life. He is not living the life he was destined to live all because he thinks he can handle the trial of his Mom's death himself. God is in hot pursuit of Sal and hopefully Sal will turn around before he ends up permanently harming himself.

Self-Observation

I have always thought I was being loving by treating other people with kindness and respect no matter their background, race or age. However, as I began to understand the importance of self-observation to see the difference in "doing" verses "being", I noticed there was a big divide between the two. My self-observation allowed me to see I was really not being loving in my thoughts and attitudes even though my actions would have suggested otherwise. Outwardly I always smiled and said hello to all those I came into contact with. However, inwardly I noticed my first thought of the person was often negative. I would notice their weight gain, messy hair or the pajamas they were wearing to Walmart. I did not have mean intentions about what I noticed but I was still sitting in a place of judgment about their outward appearance. My new awareness of how I am "being" allows me to correct and overcome the false beliefs about the importance of outward appearance that society ingrains into all of our minds. Now I guard my carnal mind and align myself with the Divine mind, noticing first the Divinity within every person.

"*The eye is the lamp of the body; so then if your eye is clear, your whole body will be full of light. But if your eye is bad, your whole body will be full of darkness. If then the light that is in you is darkness, how great is the darkness!*"

– *Hebrews 6:22-23*

LESSON 9

YOUR EYES

This verse speaks about the eyes ability to bring light into the body so that we can know the hope of God for our lives. God wants us to recognize the importance of our natural, internal and spiritual vision. What we hold in our visual fields and the perceptions we choose to see affects the co-creative process.

Here is a funny story to show you how the eyes can have such an influence. Bob's friend Stu was in town with his girlfriend and stopped by to visit. She was pretty and you couldn't help but notice her large breasts in the low-cut shirt she was wearing. During the visit, Stu asked Bob if he would be up for going out later that night. As their visit drew to a close, Bob asked "so what time do you want to hit the big titty tonight?" Obviously, Bob was letting his eyes influence his mind, so the wrong word came out instead of city!

When we look at something with our natural eyes, we can look at it indifferently, or we can look at it and have an emotion attached to what we are seeing. When there is high emotional attachment to what we are looking at, the energy level is raised significantly. As we have already discussed, like energies attract like energies. So, it is important to begin noticing what kind of emotional attachment you are giving to the things you are looking at. As an example, when your spouse or kids come home from a long day and you lay eyes on them, what do you see? What emotions arise when you look at them? If love, respect, caring, or appreciation comes to mind at the sight of them, then you are giving off positive energy. If disgust, hatred, resentment or anger surface at their sight, then you are giving them negative energy. Do you think they feel it even if you don't verbalize the emotions? Of course, they do! They are either going to be drawn toward you or will try to avoid you like the plague. What your eyes are seeing highly influences your thought. Here is another example. I know a man who when he comes home from work and he looks at his wife, his eyes light up and he tells her "I am a lucky guy." He isn't focusing on the baby weight she hasn't lost yet, or her messed up hair. He is seeing her on the outside and inside in a positive light, so his thoughts hold positive images of her. In turn she feels his positive and authentic energy and their relationship is strengthened. God is able to co-create a good relationship because of the high positive energy.

Sometimes our natural vision seems drawn to or can't get past the negative images it sees. This is when the mind's eye or the internal vision can take over and transform our negative natural vision into a positive visualization of what could be. When you visualize, you are using your internal vision to set an expectation for the things you want. Visualization is outcome based, so you visualize as if you already have whatever it is you want. If your relationship is bad, visualize what it would look like if it were really good. If you have always wanted to move into your dream house, then visualize what it looks like and see yourself living there. As with your natural eye sight, the more emotion you feel with visualization, the higher the energy frequency. So, don't only visualize but feel the emotion of your good relationship or of moving into your dream house. You then activate the law of attraction on a spiritual level.

Spiritual vision can be attained through spiritual practices. Some term this as seeing with the third eye. Spiritual vision is connecting with the God spirit within and receiving messages, comfort and visions for direction and understanding. Usually, spiritual vision comes when you are able to quiet your busy mind. Sometimes spiritual vision shows up as a vivid dream. Other times it may be a vision or thought that just pops in out of nowhere. Lately when I am lifting weights, when my mind is quiet because of the mundane repetition, God has popped in profound statements. I know they are not my own because they are stated in ways I normally would not think or talk. Meditation, yoga, prayer and other spiritual practices facilitate seeing with the third eye. When you are able to tap into spiritual vision, it is an awe-inspiring experience. It is one on one communication with The Divine. You are just that important and so loved.

Get out of God's Way

We get in the way of utilizing our gifts of vision by not recognizing the impact our vision has over our lives, therefore, not taking advantage of the gifts of vision as God intended us to use them. Frequently we fill our vision field with negative images that are not of love for ourselves or others. In turn, these visions create negative thoughts and negative energies which influence our lives in negative ways. Also, when we don't take the time to visualize the outcomes we want, we don't allow hope into our lives. Hope is "a feeling of expectation and desire for a certain thing." (Martin Luther King) Visualization lets hope in and allows God the opportunity to bring the expectations and desires of our hearts to fruition. Finally, choosing not to develop the muscle of our spiritual eye hinders our ability to "see" God's direction and guidance clearly. God has given us the gifts of vision to be the lamp of our bodies to help light our way. Use your natural, internal, and spiritual vision as they were intended to help co-create the life of your dreams!

Practice

Begin to take notice of the visual images you are allowing in and the perception of them in your thoughts. You want to align your vision with positive thought patterns. It is necessary sometimes to guard your mind from what your eyes are bringing in. Nothing can be more depressing to me than watching the nightly news. When I see tragic events, I guard my mind. I try to focus on the helpers, those people who are showing love by doing good where the bad has occurred; or I remind myself that most people are good and those who commit heinous acts must be living a hellish life on earth, so full of darkness that they can't feel God's love.

Make a vision board of anything you would like to see manifested in your life and hang it where you can see it every day. Remember that whatever you focus on with the most emotion will have higher energy attached to it and will attract people, circumstances and the energy to bring it to fruition. All you have to do is draw attention and emotion to the things you want as if they are already happening, and God does the rest. So many people don't ever have the life of their dreams because they don't ask. God wants to give you the desires of your heart. *"With man this is impossible, but with God all things are possible"* (Mathew 19:26, NIV)

Start developing your spiritual eye by getting involved with a spiritual practice. There are classes you can take and weekend seminars that teach you how to develop spiritual practices so that you can "see" God's direction more clearly.

Stories of Confirmation

My Vision Board

Honestly when I first heard of the idea of a vision board, I was very skeptical. I decided I would try it to see what would happen. I collected pictures and words of things that I would like to have in my life. Some of my pictures were material things while others were relational, or health related. I hung it up in our hallway where I could see it every day. I added things and took things down as my vision became clearer of what I wanted. I chose 3 things to give a lot of emotional attention to: a kitchen remodel, a beach vacation and improving my relationship with my husband. Then I guarded my mind from any negative thought about why I couldn't have them. To my surprise, spirit answered my request and God arranged the conditions to bring the things on my vision board about. My kids would get so excited for me as God and I co-created the things on my vision board.

The most interesting thing happened with my vision board on the first Christmas after I put it up. My youngest daughter Elle wanted Santa to bring her a camera. Since she was pretty young Santa was going to fulfill her wish with a cheap one. When I made my shopping trip, I went to Target to pick up a cheap, hot pink camera I had seen in their sale ad. I drove to Target and stood in line at the electronics counter. When it was my turn, I asked the clerk for the camera. She told me that the man in front of me had just purchased the last one. I went to other stores and could not find a cheap camera anywhere, so I headed home empty handed the day before Santa was to come. I was telling my sister about how I couldn't find Elle a camera anywhere. Santa was a little stressed because that was all she had asked for. My sister called me at noon on Christmas Eve and said that she was just in the local Walgreen's and they had a cheap camera. I quickly ran up there purchased the camera and wrapped it up for Elle. On Christmas morning as Elle opened her camera she screamed "It's just like the camera on the vision board!" I had no idea that she had cut out a picture of a camera and placed it on my vision board. She ran and pulled off a picture that was so little that I hadn't noticed it. I had purchased the exact make and model of camera from the same store ad she had put on the board. I am certain that it was no coincidence that the hot pink camera was sold or that I couldn't find another one anywhere. God wanted to manifest and finish the co-creating process that Elle started.

Visualization Miracle

When we moved to our old farmhouse, there was a real eye sore on the property. When you pulled in the drive, you first noticed an ugly lake. It was 2 ½ acres and wrapped around the whole property. It was overgrown and so silted in that there were weeds and even a tree growing out of it. My husband hated it and quickly got estimates to break the dam and dig it out. Much to his distress the estimates ran close to $20,000. We did not have that kind of money, so the eye sore would have to stay put for a long time. Day after day when he came home from work, he would get out of his car and look at the lake, then come into the house with a grumpy disposition. Days turned into weeks and then to months. Finally, it dawned on me...

I needed to teach him what Twyla had helped me understand. I told him that he had a choice to make. He could keep making himself depressed by looking at the lake, seeing its ugliness and focusing on how we didn't have the money to fix it, or he could begin to visualize what the lake was going to look like when it was fixed. I told him it was important to have faith that at the right time God would arrange for it to come to pass. It took some coaxing on my part, but he finally got tired of being depressed about it and started the visualization process.

We were still in bed early on Saturday morning a couple weeks later when we heard all this commotion outside. We jumped up to see a semi pulling in our drive loaded down with a bulldozer, track hoe and back hoe. After throwing on some clothes we got outside just as the driver was finishing unloading the equipment. He told us that he heard we needed our lake fixed. When we told him, we couldn't afford to have it done, he told us that he was there to do it for free! As we argued with him and told him that we didn't expect that, he said he had the equipment and loved doing the work. Jack owned a local construction company and he and my husband had gone to junior high and high school together. Jack worked for several days breaking the dam and knocking down trees to clear the lake. He wouldn't even let us pay for the gas for his equipment. Needless to say, we were so very grateful and we knew God had placed it upon Jack's heart to do what he did. If my husband would not have been able to visualize the finished lake, he would have prevented God from being able to manifest it. We have to do our part, so God can do what we can't!

Passing It On

As I began to understand how God was happy to co-create through visualization and vision boards, I wanted to share the information so that others could experience it for themselves. In my high school health classes there was a chapter on goal setting. I decided to incorporate vision boards and positive thinking into the chapter on goals so that my students had these tools to use throughout their lives. It was a little tricky since I was in public schools and couldn't freely talk about God. However, I was able to explain it through quantum physics and mentioned that those who believe in a "higher power" use co-creation to manifest the things they want in their lives. While I was explaining, I would bring in pictures from my vision board to display on the smart board for my students to see. As a busy mom of four, I wasn't utilizing my vision board as I should. I didn't take the time to look at my images or feel the emotion as if I already had them. Every semester when I would teach this lesson, it reminded me to really manifest what I wanted. There was always an image that I would choose to manifest while I taught. As I explained the process to each of my six hours, I really focused and brought emotion to the one thing I had chosen. Every semester for 7 years, each item I chose was manifested within a few weeks to a month after teaching the lesson. The neat thing was that I would always tell my students what I was manifesting at the moment I was teaching and then they were able to witness those things coming true for me

The kids who followed through with the process of manifesting always were successful. I had students manifest, cars, computers, better relationships with their parents, better grades, jobs, friends, money and one student won front row tickets to a Justin Bieber concert by being the 10th caller for a radio station contest! We serve an awesome God and He wants to bless you with the life of your dreams. Start visualizing!

The words you speak should be chosen with care; for they have the power to be a blessing or a curse upon your life.

– Pamela Evischi

LESSON 10

YOUR MOUTH

The mouth/tongue is such a crucial part of your body that you use to co-create. There is much power in the spoken word. The Bible talks about its importance, "*The tongue has the power of life and death, and those who love it will eat its fruit.*" (Proverbs 18:21, NIV) and also, "*For by your words you will be acquitted, and by your words you will be condemned.*" (Matthew 12:37, NIV) The words you speak can either be a blessing over your life or can be a curse. The words you say slip into the subconscious mind and attract the spoken situation. I don't know about you, but I want my words to bless my life. Therefore, when you begin to understand the power of the spoken word, you must choose your words very carefully.

When my son Charlie was in kindergarten, he won a raffle at a local picnic and his prize was an iron. The look on his face was as if he had won a million dollars. My older kids said, "you are so lucky!" Well Charlie took those words to heart and spoke them often to himself. He always would say "Write my name down. I am lucky, I will win". Charlie always has had "good luck" but it is really by his own doing through the affirmative words he has spoken to himself throughout his life. Think about the words you tell yourself daily. You manifest whatever it is you are repeating to yourself. When you wake up in the morning and you say, "I hate my job" or "I feel like crap," you are going to have situations arise during the day that justify you hating your job. By the time you get home, you will have a massive headache and really feel like crap! Do your words match the vision you have for your life? Are they a blessing over your life, or are they a curse?

Get out of Gods Way

Everyone has times when they have garbage coming out of their mouths. The important thing is to catch yourself and change your words, so you give power to those things you want in your life. Twyla really worked on me with this when I did not like my husband. I remember getting together with my sister whose marriage was near divorce and complaining about our husbands. The more I complained about my husband, the more I received what I was complaining about. I had to stop giving energy to the things that I did not want. Even though I was not happy with him, I stopped talking about the things that were making me unhappy. Instead, I talked about the things I was happy with and began to use affirmations for the things I would like to see manifested in our relationship. For example, I would speak this to myself about my husband, "He is eager to help in the raising of our children, he is a good father and husband." I would take my negative thoughts and words about him and turn them into positive, present tense power phrases. Co-creation is always taking place as long as we are thinking and speaking. Recognizing that and being mindful of what we are co-creating is where we begin to realize the blessings and abundance of God. Twyla gave me a book by Florence Shovel Shinn called, Your Word Is Your Wand, which I highly recommend. In this book, Florence talks about how to transform your words into powerful affirmations, so that God can bless you. There are examples by topic which are really useful when there is a specific area of your life you need to transform.

Practice

Notice when your words are being a curse to your life and shift them into positive affirmations. Affirmations work best when you attach positive emotions, thoughts, and actions and hand them over to God in faith. Here is a good example of a powerful affirmation, "I am fearless in letting money go out, knowing God is my immediate and endless supply." After stating this, next make sure your actions are matching your affirmation. You cannot constantly worry about money, speak of lack of money, and take actions as if there is a shortage of money. You have to boldly have faith that God will supply you.

Your speaking words are prayers over your life. Make sure those words are prayers of blessings and for positive outcomes. "*Therefore, I tell you, whatever you ask for in prayer, believe that you have received it, and it will be yours.*" (Mark 11:24, NIV) Praying is so important to developing your communication with God. If you want to have a good relationship with anyone, you have to talk to them and share your feelings. God is no different. When you pray, you are building intimacy for intrapersonal communication with God. Being able to hear God comes through prayer. Hearing His voice allows Him to direct you, so you are not misled by others. Prayer is as simple as talking to God. It is transformative. Your words uttered in prayer are direct links to the Divine. Don't be concerned about how to pray, just open your heart, and let the words flow. God will teach you how to pray. Like everything, it becomes easier with practice. The Bible tells us in 1Thessalonians 5:17 to *"pray continually,"*

which means we should be praying all day. We can do this by keeping our thoughts and spoken word on spirit, gratitude, love, and kindness and on how great God is. We can also recite prayers from our religious affiliation or even find specialty prayers online for specific things you would like prayer for.

No matter what form of prayer you decide to use, God hears them. They matter hugely to you and those you pray for. Twyla had gone to a prayer meeting and had her son Joe, prayed for. The pastor told her that Joe was in danger and to pray. She relayed the information to Joe, to be careful and to pray. The next day, a horrible feeling came over Twyla about her son Joe and she heard that she was to pray. She immediately began to pray, "Lord you said the fruit of my womb would be blessed. Please send your angels to surround Joe to protect him from harm, in Jesus's name." That same day Joe was driving his motorcycle home on wet pavement, and the back tire blew out. He was driving 80 mph, way too fast. He should have been severely injured. Instead, his motorcycle gradually laid on its side and Joe road it to a stop with a few bumps and bruises. Joe told Twyla that he knew he should have died. Those who were riding behind him said they witnessed a miracle. Prayer works! "Your words are your wand!" (Florence Shovel Shinn)

Stories of Confirmation

Believe It & Receive It

I was raised in a family who worked hard for what they had, and there were many financial struggles. My parents were thankful for what they had and never complained about not having enough money. They always thought it was ungrateful to ask for more, so they were content on just getting by OK. It was almost as if they felt unworthy to have more than what they needed. My parents unknowingly passed the mentality onto us kids. Until I met Twyla, I thought there was something wrong with abundance and was embarrassed to have nice things. During one of our talks, Twyla said, never say "there is not enough money" or "I don't have the money to buy that". She told me to say things like "abundance is mine" or "even though I can't see a way, God is in control and will make a way." Not long after my encounter with Twyla, my son came home with a shoe order form for team basketball shoes. Kenny was in 5th grade and was so excited to have made the varsity team. The team shoes were $50 and at that time in our life, that was a lot of money. Money, we didn't have. Normally I would have complained about the price or about the one-week timeframe they gave us to turn in the order, and the fact that they had to even have team shoes in grade school. I would have told Kenny we didn't have the money. Instead I acted excited about him getting team shoes and told him we would turn the order in soon. I affirmed, "God's timing is perfect, the money is on the way". Daily Kenny would ask about turning in the order. I would repeat the affirmation and tell him, "don't worry we will turn it in on time." Two days before the order was to be turned in there was a letter addressed to me in the mail. When I opened it, there was a check made out to me for $100.00 with a "Thank You" note. Two months earlier I had helped an elderly lady decorate the school gym for a party she was having. In her note she stated that she just wanted to give me a token of her appreciation for helping her. I don't know why it took her 2 months to write me a note or why she felt to give me money, but I do know God's timing and supply is perfect!

Prayer's Power

When it was time for my youngest daughter Elle to go to high school, I was feeling that she would not fair too well at the local school. I thought the best option was to enroll her in private school that was 30 miles away. This was a very big decision but one that God gave me confirmation that we should follow through with. So, even though Elle hated me for sending her to a school where she knew no one, I knew that it would be the best for her. Off she went. Every morning I would drive her 10 miles to catch the bus that would take her the rest of the way to school. Then after her sport practice, every night for two years until she got her driver's license, I would make the one-hour round trip drive to get her home. Every day I worried about if she was going to adjust OK. I always received signs of confirmation letting me know that this decision would be a blessing for her. As the first few weeks of school passed by, both of us started feeling better. The girls on her volleyball team were all going to the Homecoming dance together and invited her to go with them. Elle was so excited. The night of the dance she got all dolled up went for dinner, and pictures, and then to the dance. At around 9:30, Elle called me and asked me to come and pick her up and to hurry. When Elle got into the car she just sobbed. All the girls on her team ignored her all night and wouldn't talk to her. When she approached the group, they would all turn and walk away. She was devastated, and I felt horrible. I began to pray saying "God you said that this school would be a blessing for Elle. Please move to make it so." "Please bring a great friend into her life soon to make her feel welcomed and a part of the school". Of course, the following Monday, she dreaded going back to school. I tried to keep positive and told her that it just takes time to make friends, especially since most of them had grown up together and attended the same local grade school. Elle was a trooper and put a smile on her face and headed off to school. The next few weeks had its ups and downs, but after a month, things began to change. Let me just say, I was praying without ceasing! A girl named Cheyenne from Elle's team was really being nice to her. Normally Elle went to the library after school to study for an hour while she was waiting for practice to start. Cheyenne started inviting her to come over to her house after school to do their homework together. Cheyenne's family was awesome, one of the most respected families in town and were just really good people. Cheyenne's acceptance of the new girl at school caused her some problems with her friends who weren't too excited to have Elle hang out with them. However, Cheyenne always included Elle in any plans she had with other girls. In fact, sometimes the other girls would not invite Elle, so Cheyenne chose to hang out with Elle instead of following the crowd. Eventually Elle and Cheyenne became best friends and the other girls also accepted Elle in large part because of Cheyenne's stamp of approval. She and her family were the answer to my prayers. God didn't just bring Elle a good friend. He went above and beyond, Elle got a second family who always allowed her to hang out at their house when she didn't have time to get home, when the bus got in late on game nights, or when the weather was bad. Cheyenne's mom, Stacey is like a second mother to her. Elle has always had the comfort to know that if she got sick at school or needed anything, Stacey was only 5 minutes away. Cheyenne and her entire family have been such a wonderful blessing in our lives. We are forever grateful that God answers prayers!

Money Magnet

I had a student who chose the affirmation "I am a money magnet". This student lived in the local children's home. Lacy was 15, so she didn't have a job and did not have any financial support from family. She pretty much depended on the children's home for the things that she needed. Just like any teenager, Lacy wanted some money to give her a little more freedom to do and buy things the children's home didn't provide. Each day before class, I would have my students repeat their affirmation to themselves. I reminded them to feel with emotion as if they already had what they wanted. I would usually give it a good week before I asked the kids if any of their affirmations were coming to fruition. One day right after the bell rang, Lacy stood up and threw her arms up in victory shouting "I am a money magnet!" Everyone laughed and wanted to know what happened. She stated that she had been repeating her affirmation many times as she was going through her days. The previous night, the team leader at the children's home had taken a bunch of kids to Walmart. The leader told Lacy she could pick out a box of ice cream treats for the group. Lacy went over to the freezer grabbed a box of fudge pops and behind the box was a twenty-dollar bill! She said, "Mrs. Evischi, I took that $20 and said, I am a money magnet, shoved it in my pocket and said, thank you for my abundance." Lacy was beaming from ear to ear. God was showing her that no matter what her circumstance, He was there and willing to co-create with her. My wish for my students always is for them to get a glimpse of God's love so that it might make them curious about him and motivate them to begin seeking him.

God's Supply in His Time

I love to teach because it gives me an opportunity to be a positive influence in kids' lives. At the high school level, I saw so many lost, broken spirited and struggling teens. I did my best to try awakening my students to something more without mentioning God. However, it was very frustrating working in public schools because I could not teach the things that I was so passionate about, something I knew would so benefit my students. In my sixth year, I began to feel that I would not be teaching there much longer. I wasn't sure how this was going to play out since I had 3 kids in college and 1 in a private high school. My paycheck was very important to making ends meet. I just said to God, "If it is your will that I leave this job, please make it known to me". Two months after the next school year started, my husband received a little raise. Shortly after, he told me that if I wanted to quit my job at the end of the school year that we could probably make ends meet even though it would be tight. Of course, I was excited at the prospect of following my dream of teaching people about God. At the same time, I was worried about losing my salary for the family. My biggest concern was that losing my salary would put too much of a financial burden on my husband, and that he would begin to resent me for quitting my job. I began to pray and asked for confirmation from God if it was His will for me to quit. I received confirmation, so I put my faith in God that He would work everything out and decided to follow Spirit.

In the meantime, there was a job opening at work that my husband had always talked about wanting. If he got it, we would not have any financial worries. In his current job, he had absorbed the work load of another employee who had retired and was given a new title but was not given a pay increase. So, I was excited that this might be the reward for all his hard work. As the time approached for him to put in his application, he didn't do it. I was frustrated with him knowing that the loss of my salary would not matter if he would just apply for the job. I knew he would get it. I was also afraid that God had set up the opportunity for him and he wasn't following through. We had a few heated discussions about it. He stood his ground saying he had changed his mind and did not want the stress that came with the position. I have learned to just turn my frustrations over to God letting His will be done, so that was what I did. I continued to pray for God to work everything out.

I waited until the last two weeks of school before I told my boss I would not be returning the next school year. The most amazing thing happened while I was turning in my resignation. At approximately the same time, my husband's boss called him on the phone and informed him that his position had been re-evaluated and he would be getting a pay increase to reflect the current job market. He received a

$20,000 pay increase. It was 2 years overdue but in God's perfect timing. Now that was the confirmation that I was making the right decision! His raise didn't replace my salary, but it sure helped and made me more at ease. It also showed me once again, that when you follow spirit, God fights your battles for you and supplies your needs. God is good!

"And my God will meet all your needs according to the riches of his glory in Christ Jesus. To our God and Father be the glory for ever and ever. Amen."

– Philippians 4:19-20

LESSON 11

GOD NEVER SAYS NO

An important thing to remember about the co-creative process is that God never tells us no. Sometimes when we don't see something manifested right away or in the way we think it should be, we begin to doubt or think that God is telling us no. Twyla was always reminding me that everything happens in God's time and not our own. When you co-create, you have to let go of the results and allow God to show you his favor. Sometimes God responds with a resounding yes, and you get whatever you wanted. At other times, God might not act right away because certain things have to align correctly in order for the manifesting to occur. If my husband had gotten upset that he didn't get the raise he deserved when he got his promotion, he would have interrupted the plan that God had, which was two years in the making

Many times, God's answer is "I have a better idea". God knows the plan he has for our lives, and although we might want to manifest one thing, God might have something better for us that we have not even considered. This happens a lot in relationships. I have heard many couples talk about how a break up of one relationship was a blessing in hind sight because God brought a better partner into their lives. So it is important to remember that there is always a greater plan for why things happen the way they do. In those times of trial or doubt, guard your mind and be patient knowing that the silver lining is just around the corner.

Twyla has a cousin Lonnie, who has had the gift of prophesy since he was a young man. When he is given a name, he is given a prophetic word that is relevant to what is happening in their life. He says that over all of the years of hearing from God, the message he gets the most for people is for them to "wait upon the Lord". In our "I want it now" society, this is difficult for many to do. However, if you force the outcome you want, it never works out for your highest good. It also can lead to making hasty choices that will end up having less than desirable consequences. Over the years, Lonnie has had many people call for a word about their health issues. Often, he is just given words of encouragement, but sometimes he will get that they are to wait and not go to a doctor because God will heal them in his time. However, because of fear and lack of faith sometimes they end up going to the doctor, and then major complications arise, or they die. Twyla was one of those who was told not to go to the doctor. She had faith and has not seen a doctor even though she is very sick. If she would have gone to the doctor, I know that she would have already been dead. Not because doctors are bad or because I don't believe in them, but because of her condition, they would have medicated her and put her in a nursing home, crushing her spirit. Instead, God has a greater plan. Even though she has been bedridden for 10 years, she has never had one bedsore! That is a sign of someone who is hearing God. She gets better and better, and he has used the illness to grow her spiritually and to allow her to minister to others.

It's been my experience that God uses the waiting process for two reasons. First, we may need to make some changes in our thinking or actions to align with the plan God has for our lives. So, when you feel like you are in a rut or spinning your wheels in some area of your life, reflect and see if you are doing anything to impede God's progress in those areas. I couldn't fully step into the plans God had for my life until I was willing to stop people pleasing and worrying about what everyone else thought. Secondly, sometimes God is preparing you for the future plan he has for your life. For instance, if your purpose is to be the president of a company and right now you are an entry level employee, you would be unprepared to be a successful president if you were promoted all the way to the top today. During God's waiting process, He will put people, circumstances and trials in your life to prepare and teach you what you need to know. That way you are ready for His future plan for your life. So, while you wait, keep in mind that God's timing is perfect. Keep faith throughout any trial you may incur knowing His ways are for your highest good. He is the God of miracles. While you wait, live fully in and appreciate the present. Wait with joyful expectation knowing that God is in control.

A word of caution as you awaken to the co-creation process, keep your eyes on God! Remember that when we take our eyes off of Him, the dark side of humanness can overtake the process. Feelings of entitlement, thinking we can do it on our own, forgetting to give God the glory, creating other gods of wealth, possessions and power remove us from His holy flow of creation and hinder our personal relationship with Him.

As you keep your eye on him and co-create with God, you will eventually come to a place of humility and awe seeing how much God loves and cares about you. I believe God co-creates with us to move us into a higher spiritual awareness and greater understanding of His ways. Cocreation is a place of surrender when we invite God into our everyday lives. When we begin to want what God wants for our life, we begin to place our trust in Him in all areas of our life. We begin to replace worry and fear with an unwavering knowledge that God is in control with our best interest in mind. We begin to live more often in a place of love, peace and joy. We begin to understand the responsibility in our co-creative role in furthering His kingdom of love. We strive to get up each day filled with gratitude and wanting to be used by Him to uplift and encourage those we come into contact with. Maybe it is through a kind word, a smile, a good deed or just by letting the light of God shine forth from you- uplifting an entire room just by your presence.

Stories of Confirmation:

15 Years to Fruition

It has been fifteen years since I first turned around to answer God's call and began my supernatural, spiritual journey. Back then, I felt called to teach others the spiritual lessons I was learning, however, it wasn't the time yet. I was a busy mom of four; I didn't have the time to devote to anything except my family. I knew what I wanted to be doing, but knew it had to be in God's timing. During this season in my life, I often felt frustrated. I had to wait. However, the waiting was not in vain. During those years, God continued to show me more, expand me spiritually, and prepare me for His future plans. I had to keep my eyes on Him and place my trust in Him knowing that in the right divine time, He would make the way.

Going It Alone

I know a really good guy who has grown up in church but has never put his faith in God where his career is concerned. He has been in and out of different jobs his whole life. He will hear about a new job opportunity and talk about how great it is going to be, but never takes the time to ask God if it is in the divine plan for his life. Soon after, he quickly realizes that the new job is not what he expected and is not happy in his work. When the next opportunity arises, he impulsively jumps at it only to repeat the same results. When I try to talk to him about asking God about what he should do, he just laughs and is condescending. He thinks he can do life by himself and that God is an "out there" God. He can't wrap his head around God's willingness to partner with him to co-create his life. Because of this, he and his family have struggled because of dissatisfaction and financial instability in his work. All he has to do is ask God, then follow through on His guidance, and the outcome would be very different. It is so important and fun to ask God about every endeavor in our lives. When we heed his direction, we are choosing to live in the flow of spirit and He leads us to success and happiness.

A Better Idea

When I was going through the struggles in my marriage, I often felt hopeless. I felt that because of the great distance between me and my husband, there was no way it could be a successful and happy marriage. All sorts of ideas ran through my carnal mind, ranging from disappearing never to be found, to doing nothing and just staying in an unhappy relationship because of the kids. In my desperation, I remember even asking God to send a pretty seductress my husband's way so I could have a way out.

However, Twyla's lessons began to take root in me, and I began to take action. I guarded my mind, I used visualization, I spoke victory over my marriage, and I prayed for a change in my husband and myself. On tough days, I would ask for spiritual assistance, whether it was for a sign of confirmation that God was working everything out or for arranging meetings with people or circumstances to show me God's favor and support.

As I took action, God started transforming me and guiding my spiritual evolution. As I evolved and my energy moved toward The Light, all things around me had to evolve also or move away from my space. At the time, I wasn't sure which way my husband would move, but I had faith that God had the perfect plan for my life. As I kept seeking God, I noticed my husband slowly began to change in areas where I thought he never would. Interestingly, he made the changes by his own choice without me having to nag or even ask.

Today I am so grateful that my husband and I chose to stick out the rough patch in our marriage and to turn to God for help. God had a better idea; one I thought was out of reach. He helped bring about changes in both of us so that He could co-create with us a happy, fulfilling, and loving marriage.

P.S. If your marriage is in trouble, invite God in to your life and use these tools as a springboard for your spiritual growth. You can't change your spouse, you can only change yourself. Invite God in and he can change both of you, re-create and restore your marriage!

"My religion consists of a humble admiration of the illimitable superior spirit who reveals himself in the slight details we are able to perceive with our frail and feeble mind."

– Albert Einstein

God's Letter to You

My Dearest Child,

You are perfectly and wonderfully made. Yes, you, the one who is reading this. I knew you before you were born and set you apart from all others to be here at this exact time. I have equipped you with everything you need to fulfill the purpose for your time here. You have been graced with unique talents and capabilities that only you possess. I am in you, as you are a spark off of my Divine Flame. Everything you need is right inside you. Nothing is impossible. I am the God of Miracles.

Do not be afraid, for I am with you always, in the highest of highs and the deepest of deeps. When you are weak, I am strong. Lean on me for understanding, knock and the door shall be opened for you. Ask and you shall receive. Right now, the Divine Plan is playing out in your life. Have the faith of a mustard seed, knowing that all things work together for your highest good. I have the plan for your life. I hold you in My Hands. Stop with the worry and fearful thinking! For these occupy the minds of those who are asleep. Wake up and place your trust in me. I will fulfill all your needs and the desires of your heart.

Begin today to accept my favor. Let the love, peace, and joy that I have placed within you pour out in your mind, words, and actions. Cast your burdens upon Me and lighten your step. Be My partner in the divine dance of life. Let go of the need to control. I will guide you and lead you into a life more magnificent than you could ever imagine. Place your eyes and heart on me; enter the divine and loving flow of your birthright. You are a child of the Most High, step into your destiny!

With my unconditional love for you always,

Your Father, God

THIS IS JUST THE BEGINNING...

I would like to share the story of the preceding letter. On two consecutive nights God came to me in a dream. He first asked me to write a letter for Him as a reminder and encouragement to His Children. In the second dream I told him that I had no business writing a letter for Him. He told me that He would tell me what to write and then proceeded to do just that. "God's Letter to You" comes directly from Him. I am honored to be the messenger for this wonderful letter. I hope it makes a difference in your life.

I am so excited for what lies ahead for you. I hope I have sparked your curiosity enough to get you to apply these simple tools and practices to your daily life. God wants to be your everyday God; your strength, your comforter, your joy, your all-in-all. You are the apple of His eye and He longs to show you His unconditional love and favor. All you have to do to experience His supernatural presence in your own life is to take ACTION. Turn around to God's pursuit, partner with Him, get out of His way and let Him springboard your life into a whole new spiritual dimension. It will be the best choice you ever make.

For added support & encouragement
visit Spiritualspringboard.com

www.ingramcontent.com/pod-product-compliance
Lightning Source LLC
Chambersburg PA
CBHW071403290426
44108CB00014B/1662